DC

JUSTI

DO JUSTICE

Linking Christian Faith
and
Modern Economic Life

REBECCA M. BLANK

United Church Press
Cleveland, Ohio

United Church Press, Cleveland, Ohio 44115

Scripture quotations are from the New Revised Standard Version Bible, copyright 1989, Division of Christian Education of the National Council of the Churches of Christ in the United States of America, and are used by permission.

Printed in the United States of America on acid-free paper.

96 95 94 93 92   5 4 3 2 1

Library of Congress Cataloging-in-Publication Data

Blank, Rebecca M.
    Do justice : linking Christian faith and modern economic
life / Rebecca M. Blank.
        p. cm.
    ISBN 0-8298-0929-5 (alk. paper)
    1. Economics—Religious aspects—Christianity. I. Title.
BR115.E3B57 1992
261.8'5—dc20   91-48104
                                                      CIP

And what does the LORD require of you but to
do justice, and to love kindness, and to walk
humbly with your God?

–Micah 6:8

Contents

Acknowledgments

This book has emerged out of the efforts by the United Church of Christ (UCC) to gather a diverse group of persons for discussion, argument, and prayer over the issues of economics and theology. I have been fortunate enough to participate in many of these gatherings, and I am indebted to all members of the group who collaborated in producing the study paper "Christian Faith and Economic Life" (edited by Audrey Chapman), particularly the two chairpersons of that process, Douglas Meeks and James Weaver. I also thank all persons who were faithfully involved in the writing and revising of *A Pronouncement on Christian Faith: Economic Life and Justice*, passed at the United Church of Christ's General Synod 17 in July 1989. As author of this book, I have used the ideas that percolated through many of the discussions of these earlier documents. To all of the participants in these earlier sessions, I owe enormous thanks.

Over the years I have worked particularly closely with two UCC staff persons, Charles McCollough and Audrey Chapman. I have come to value their friendship and to admire and trust their insights. I owe both of them an enormous debt of gratitude for their support in this endeavor and for the model they have provided through their own commitments to economic justice issues.

I want to thank the three instrumentalities in the United Church of Christ that have supported the work within the UCC attempting to develop a linkage between economics and theology: the Board for World Ministries, the Board for Homeland Ministries, and the Office for Church in Society (OCIS). A wide variety of staff members from these organizations have given moral, practical, and political support to these efforts through the years. I particularly thank Yvonne Delk for her leadership role as executive director of OCIS; her efforts assured the completion of the *Pronouncement*.

This book itself has been written over the last year under the sponsorship of the OCIS committee charged with implementing the *Pronouncement,* headed by Charles McCollough. I thank Charles McCollough, Bill Webber, and Jim McDaniel, who serve on this committee and who read the first draft of this book and provided very helpful comments. I also thank Dan McAdams and Peter Moll, two colleagues at Northwestern University, who made valuable comments on the first draft. In addition, I appreciate the support, comments, and editorial guidance of Barbara Withers, James Heaney, and the staff of the Pilgrim Press.

I thank my parents, whose own commitments to justice have been a model throughout my life. And I thank all those friends in the communities of faith where I have been nurtured and where my ideas of faith and justice have been formed:

Falcon Heights United Church of Christ, St. Paul,
  Minnesota
The United Church of Hyde Park, Chicago, Illinois
First Church in Cambridge, Congregational (UCC),
  Cambridge, Massachusetts
Christ Congregation, Princeton, New Jersey
First Congregational Church (UCC), Washington, D.C.
St. Paul's United Church of Christ, Chicago, Illinois

A comment on the statistics cited in this book is necessary. Because this book is largely intended for a nonacademic audience, it does not contain footnotes or extensive citations. Unless otherwise noted in the text, all statistics for the United States come from official U.S. government sources. All numbers regarding income and poverty in the United States are from the two recent publications, *Money Income of Households, Families, and Persons in the United States, 1990* and *Poverty in the United States, 1990,* published by the U.S. Department of Commerce, Bureau of the Census (Series P-60, Nos. 174 and 175). For international statistics, the text typically indicates the organization or source of the numbers. Anyone desiring more complete references for specific numbers should contact the author.

Economics and the Church

We all have some experience with economic pain and suffering in our lives. Some of us struggle daily with economic need. Even those among us who have found economic security for the present are rarely free from the fear that unemployment or disability or death or divorce may threaten that security. Most of us have struggled at times with too many bills to pay and too little cash. Many have faced the end of a job or the failure of a business. Many have agonized over difficult choices in order to balance the budget for our family, our business, or our local church. Many have felt the pain of being excluded from economic opportunities because of skin color, sex, ethnic background, physical disabilities, or sexual orientation.

We all carry within us some combination of personal and community memories that recall the struggles experienced by ourselves, our parents, our children, and our friends and neighbors amid uncertain jobs, rising prices, discrimination, growing family needs, and inadequate income. Many of us can tell the family story of economic success or economic failure, as it occurred to us, to our parents, and to our grandparents. Our relative American affluence may make our stories of economic change seem insignificant next to the desperate struggle with poverty that our neighbors in other countries could talk about, yet our own stories and these memories provide us with a touchstone to help us remain sensitive to the pain of poverty and unemployment and human need wherever it occurs.

The Response of the Church

The church has always responded to human pain brought about by economic suffering. Throughout its history, the church has tried to be a supportive community that lives out God's love by helping those who struggle with the world's uncertainties to retain a sense of self-worth and hope in the midst of their struggles. The church has also actively preached the necessity of providing material assistance to those in need and has lived that message by implementing a wide range of outreach projects, from local soup kitchens and quiet help for individual members to the establishment of major worldwide assistance organizations such as Church World Service.

Yet, even while the church has worked to alleviate economic suffering, it has in many cases done little to help its members understand how their economic lives relate to their church lives. Although our churches have long since discarded any belief that economic success is a reflection of God's favor, they have not adequately articulated an alternative way of interpreting the economic suffering—as well as the economic success—in our lives and in the lives of our neighbors in the light of our faith. The study of economics and economic systems is given over to the secular world of the university and is no longer the domain of the church. But in giving the authority to understand and analyze the economy over to economists, the church gives up much of its authority to speak about economic matters. The role of the church in economic affairs becomes "after-the-fact"—after economic disruption or after suffering has occurred, the church may be called in to ease the resulting pain and to provide assistance. But "before-the-fact," when economic decisions are being made or economic institutions designed, the church is neither expected to understand nor to contribute to the discussion.

Not everyone has accepted this division of responsibility. Many faithful Christians have combined assistance to individuals with attention to the institutional structures and public policies that affect economic well-being. For instance, many church-related groups actively work to assure that government programs intended to offset economic suffering are effectively designed and adequately funded. The United Church of Christ, like many other churches, maintains an office and a staff in Washington, D.C., keeps in touch with national decision makers, and works with similarly concerned groups to shape public policy. However, the authority for this work is regularly questioned both within and outside the church. From what authority does the church speak about economics?

It has become increasingly important for the church to make explicit the links between Christian faith and economic life–to develop a Christian perspective on economics. Faithful people need to understand how their religious call to a God-centered life relates to their secular involvement in the economic systems and decisions of this world. Church institutions need to be reinvested with the authority to address economic matters.

Linking Christian faith and economic life requires that we look at the process by which economic decisions are made through the perspective of our faith, which means confronting the operation of the economy with the vision of human purpose and human society to which we are called as God's faithful people. This means we must have a common understanding of how we interpret God's intentions through our biblical and religious traditions. We also need to understand how both individual and institutional economic decisions are made in our society: We need to understand the economic life and the economic systems of our world.

The Background for This Book

Recognizing the need to think more clearly about issues of individual and institutional economies, the United Church of Christ in 1983 commissioned a group of theologians, economists, pastors, business persons, and others to write a "public theology of economics." This action spawned six years of work on a study paper, public forums on the issue of Christian faith and economic life throughout the church, much public and private debate and discussion, and, finally, the presentation of the *Pronouncement on Christian Faith: Economic Life and Justice* to General Synod 17 in July 1989. The General Synod adopted this *Pronouncement* with an overwhelmingly positive vote, becoming the first major religious body to adopt a comprehensive theological statement on faith, economics, and economic justice at a broadly representative national convention.

This action on the part of the United Church of Christ reflects a growing interest in this subject throughout the Christian church. In 1986 the National Conference of Catholic Bishops released a pastoral letter on Catholic social teaching and the U.S. economy, *Economic Justice for All*. The Presbyterian church has written a major study document, and other American denominations are writing and/or discussing these issues at different levels in their churches. In the past several years, the World Council of Churches has commissioned a group to put together material on this topic and has published several related books. Academic theologians are likewise becoming increasingly interested, and a growing number of theological books on the subject have been published in recent years.

This book emerges from the discussions that led to the *Pronouncement* adopted by the United Church of Christ in 1989. (The text of the *Pronouncement* is reprinted in the Appendix.) The book is designed to provide an expanded discussion of the economic and faith issues presented in that document, which is necessarily a terse and condensed statement. It is written both for the members of the United Church of Christ who want to learn more about the issues raised in the *Pronouncement*, as well as for members of other churches who are struggling to link their economic lives with their faith.

Although designed primarily as a religious statement, this book is written by a nontheologian, addressing other nontheologians. The author is an economist and lay church member, who has been involved in the discussions within the United Church of Christ over the past eight years. Both theologians and economists tend to speak in the vocabulary of their own particular disciplines, which are often unintelligible to those not professionally trained in these fields. This book has been written in the hope that it will be read and used by the vast majority of church members who are neither economists nor theologians.

The book is designed to be used not just by individuals who want to read more about its topic, but for adult education groups as well. At the end of each chapter are a number of study questions and exercises that can be adapted to groups of various sizes. A list of suggestions for further reading is also included at the end of the book.

An Overview

The first four chapters of this book provide a framework for linking economic decisions with Christian faith. The first chapter discusses the interconnectedness between economic decisions and faith issues. Chapter 2 discusses what the Bible says about economic justice. The experiences of economic injustice and pain in today's world are presented in chapter 3. Chapter 4 builds on both the biblical concern with economic suffering as well as our modern experiences with economic injustice to develop a set of guidelines for economic justice. Ten "Marks of a Just Economy" are presented and discussed, providing a faith-based measure by which we can evaluate our own economic system.

The next two chapters look at how economic decision making occurs in our society. Chapter 5 is designed to help a noneconomist understand the market economy of the United States. Chapter 6 presents a similar discussion of the world economy, focusing on the issues of economic development and growth among poorer nations.

Finally, the last four chapters discuss how faith and economic concerns come together in the various parts of our lives. Chapter 7 focuses on the individual lifestyle issues that confront faithful people who try to apply their faith commitments to their economic lives. Chapter 8 discusses the institutional lifestyle issues that the church must address if it is to demonstrate publicly its concern for economic pain and injustice. Chapter 9 focuses on public policy issues and addresses the question "How can our Christian concern for economic pain and injustice be translated into actions designed to reform and transform our economic and political institutions?" Chapter 10 discusses the barriers that individuals and churches must confront if they are to work toward personal, institutional, or social change. An Epilog concludes the book.

CHAPTER 1
Economic Life in God's Household

One of the fundamental claims of the Christian church is that God is present in all spheres of life. God is not with us only at certain times and places. Rather, all aspects of our life—our work, our church involvements, our family relationships—are subject to God's judgment and to God's grace. On the one hand, this means that we cannot escape the question "What is God's will in this situation?" in any of our activities. God's concern and God's judgment are ever-present. On the other hand, this means that the transforming presence of the Holy Spirit is with us in all our activities, and that there is no situation in which we cannot call upon and expect God's help.

Of course, such claims do not exclude the economic sphere of life. As discussed in the next chapter, the God we worship is as deeply concerned with the economy of God's people as with their spiritual well-being. The economic activities in which we engage are a vitally important part of our lives. As such, they reflect our faith (or our lack of faith) as much as do our Sunday morning worship activities. Some of these economic activities are considered here:

Work. How do we make our money? Work, which provides income for ourselves and our families, is a central commitment in most people's lives. Our jobs are important, not just because they provide us with money, but also because they often provide us with a sense of self-identity, establishing who we are in relation to our friends, our family, and our community. One of the first questions we ask when meeting someone new is, "What do you do?" Many of us spend more hours at paid work than at any other activity (except perhaps sleep) and many of our friends are also colleagues in our work. Throughout our lives we make a series of important economic work decisions that shape the way we live: "What job do I want?" "Should I quit work while my children are young?" "Should I go back to school?" "If I take responsibility for this project, is the extra money worth the time away from my family?" "What should I do when I'm unfairly treated on the job?" All of these are fundamental economic decisions—but all of them are also faith decisions, requiring that we decide how God calls us to live our lives.

Spending Money. How do we spend our money? The economic purpose of work is to provide income to buy the material goods necessary for our lives. Many Americans are able to make choices about what they will buy and how much they will buy. We must decide which products to buy among the many on the grocery store shelves. We must decide how much we will spend on ourselves and our own family, and how much we will give to our church or to other organizations. We must decide how much we will spend today and how much we will save for future needs. These choices are both economic decisions and fundamental lifestyle decisions that reflect our struggle to define our responsibilities to ourselves, to our family, and to our larger community.

Church Budgets. How does our local church collect and spend its money? Within most Protestant churches, church members share responsibility for running the local church. The annual congregational meeting held in many churches is the place where budgets are adopted and church policy is set. The economic decisions involved in setting a church budget mirror many of the decisions we make in determining our family budgets. How much money will we spend on our local church, and how much will we give to outside projects? How do we decide how much to spend on education versus music? How much should we pay our minister (or secretary or janitor) to compensate him or her adequately for the work required? These are hard economic decisions, as anyone knows who has ever worked on a church budget, but they are also decisions that shape the ministry of the church among its members and in the community.

Government Spending. How will our local and national communities tax us and spend our tax dollars? All U.S. citizens can be active participants in the political decisions of their local, state, or national government. It is true that in the political arena we elect representatives who act for us in making budget decisions, but who these representatives are and the decisions they make are directly affected by our opinions and activities as citizens. We have to decide whether to vote for a bond issue that will raise our property taxes and expand the local schools. We have to decide whether to support the state senate candidate who wants to initiate a state lottery to raise revenues. We have to decide whether we are going to take the time to write our U.S. representative about his or her vote on proposed changes in Social Security. Certainly, there are noneconomic issues that are also important in the public arena, but the economic choices are many and directly determine how society uses and shares the resources of its members.

None of the decisions we make in any of these areas are separate from our Christian commitments. Our faith informs both our personal economic behavior and the decisions we make that affect the economy of the larger institutions (religious or political) to which we belong.

Our Authority to Speak About Economics

Simply acknowledging that our economic lives and our faith lives are linked may not be enough to help us make "faithful" economic decisions. We must also understand something about the economy in which we live, how economic decisions are made, and how economic injustices may be created and perpetuated. Many who acknowledge the validity of the church's concern with economic issues often avoid getting involved with these issues out of a sense that the economic system is too complex, that economics can be understood only by the experts.

Yet we are all involved in our economy and we all make daily economic decisions. As a result, most persons probably understand more about economics than they might initially believe. Although many economic textbooks may seem overcomplex (if not downright unreadable to most people), this does not mean that the economy cannot be understood by those who participate in it. In fact, most persons have some understanding of the forces that shape the economy and affect their lives. Claiming that only the experts—the economists—can understand and speak about the economy is as dangerous as claiming that only theologians can understand and speak about God.

The personal faith experiences of individual Christians provide insight and understanding into the nature of God, giving lay church members authority to participate in the worship and educational work of the church. In a similar way, personal economic experiences provide insight into the problems and promises of our economic system and give individuals the authority to speak about their economic concerns. There is knowledge and authority shared by all of us who are daily participants in this economy, working, buying, and budgeting. We can validly criticize or praise this economic system as it affects our lives. Those who have experienced economic pain or economic injustice have authority to speak about their suffering. The church and its members need to claim this authority as they address economic issues.

Defining Economics in a New (Old) Way

Economics often seems confusing because of the technical way in which it is defined and discussed. Economics textbooks typically present the following definition of economics: Economics is the study of the allocation of scarce resources among competing needs. This technical definition of economics is a useful statement for professors in a university department of economics who seek to understand the functioning of a particular economic system.

This book, however, is not an economics textbook and we are (largely) not economists. For our purposes, this definition is not satisfactory. Instead, we seek a definition of economics that relates economic life to our fundamental faith assumptions about God's intention for human society. Thus, in this book we will use a definition of economics similar to that presented in the United Church of Christ *Pronouncement*, a definition that grows out of an older understanding of economics.

The word economics is derived from the Greek word, *oikonomos*, which is the combination of two words. *Oikos* means "household" and *nomos* is "the word," or "the law." *Oikonomos*, or economics, can therefore be interpreted as "the law or the management of the household."

The imagery of the household is a familiar one for Christians, for it is present throughout the Bible. The word household appears in both the Old and New Testaments. Its most familiar use to Christians may be in the steward parables of Jesus, in which Jesus tells of stewards who mismanage their households and bring forth the judgment of their masters. In the Old Testament the "household" that is referred to is typically the household of Israel. In the New Testament, however, the household is vastly expanded to include all people. The neighbor becomes not just the one next door, but the one in need, whatever his or her ethnic background. Even the Samaritan (the Russian, the Iraqi) is a neighbor to those who follow Christ. It is this uncomfortably inclusive household of God that we are called to manage.

Economics is specifically concerned with a particular aspect of household management: the distribution of the physical resources of the household. Those who have access to the physical resources of the household are assured of survival. They are given life. Those who are denied access to the physical resources of the household face exclusion, poverty, and malnourishment. They are denied life. It is not enough for Christians to define economics in a morally neutral way as "the allocation of scarce resources." Our faith gives us a moral context out of which we are called to affirm a stronger, positive statement. As Christians, we are called to provide life to all within our household. Thus, for the Christian, *economics can be defined as the management of God's household so that all may have life.*

Managing God's household so that all receive life implicitly emphasizes the need to care particularly for the well-being of the poor. As we shall see in the next chapter, the Bible again and again points out God's special concern and care for the poor. In making economic decisions, it is for those whose livelihood is most threatened that we should be most concerned. Thus, our economic decisions must always involve the question "What will this do for the poor among us?" Policies that limit the access of individuals and groups to the resources and opportunities of the larger household (economy) are a mismanagement of God's economy and are unjust. Indeed, the most effective way of "seeing" economic injustice in our world is to observe the world through the eyes of those who have been excluded from the economic abundance received by middle- and upper-income Americans.

Jesus Christ came so that "they may have life, and have it abundantly [John 10:10]." Abundant life for the Christian surely has a spiritual context; abundant life cannot occur for an individual who feels separated from God's love and mercy. But abundant life is not solely spiritual. To live abundantly one must first have access to the necessities of physical life, including food, drink, and shelter. Abundant life also requires a community, a place where an individual can find human love and concern. In short, abundant life requires the effective functioning of the entire household. To follow Jesus and to preach the good news is to be concerned with all aspects of our community life together, spiritual, physical, and interpersonal.

Managing God's Household

We are called to manage God's household—to be God's agents in a world filled with economic choices. As such, *economic life and economic justice are a central and necessary concern for a people of faith.* It is a valid Christian calling for an individual and for the church to be actively engaged in the struggle to reform and transform the economy so that it may provide all human beings with the access to livelihood and abundant life.

This is not a task we undertake alone. We will constantly need God's help as we seek to transform our individual lives and to work for greater justice in the structure of our economic and political institutions. It is only because we are assured of the presence of the Holy Spirit and the mercy of God that we dare undertake the task.

Summary

All aspects of our economic life are related to our faith, including work decisions, spending decisions, personal and church budget decisions, and citizenship activities. Since all of us participate in the economy, all of us have authority to criticize and to praise the economic structures and the economic life we share. One way to view economics from a faith perspective is to see the economy as our shared household, and economics as the management of this household so that all may have life. This definition emphasizes the need to be particularly concerned for the well-being of the poor among us.

GROUP DISCUSSION AND ACTIVITIES

Suggested Group Exercise

Divide into pairs. Tell each other your own personal economic stories, from the experiences of your grandparents through your own and those of your children. Discuss how these personal economic histories have shaped your lives: where you live, what you do, how you view the world.

Returning to the larger group, some individuals may want to tell of how their families' economic history has shaped their present lives. In the larger group, discuss: How have our individual economic backgrounds affected our religious commitments and our faith perspectives?

Starting Discussion Questions

1. Ask group members to think of one major economic decision they have made over the past year (a new job, a move, a decision about children or parents, for example). How did faith commitments affect that decision? In what ways was this decision a faith decision as well as an economic decision?

2. How does the image of the "economy" as the "household" affect the way you think about economics? What connotations does the word household have that the word economy does not? How do you respond to the definition of economics as "the management of God's household so that all may have life"?

3. How many words can you think of that have both religious and economic connotations? (examples: save, debt).

CHAPTER 2

What Does the Bible Say About Economics?

The Bible tells of God's presence in human history. Through the stories in the Bible, we acquire an understanding of what it means to be God's people—who God is, who we are, and what God requires of us. The Bible reveals to us the many aspects of God by telling how God works in this world, creating, judging; bringing justice, salvation, and mercy. The Bible tells how human beings have responded to God's presence, God's demands, and God's teachings. In sometimes simple and sometimes complex ways the Bible makes clear that those who seek to avoid God often end up in the belly of the whale. But those who hunger and thirst for righteousness find living water to quench their thirst.

The Bible is a central resource as we struggle to understand what it means to call ourselves Christian and to interpret Jesus' teachings and God's demands within our modern communities. It is not, of course, the only resource. We use our own experiences and those of others around us. We also turn to the wisdom of prophets and leaders (from Martin Luther to Martin Luther King Jr.) who have relied on their faith to find a way through difficult times. In Christian communities, however, the Bible is used most frequently as the primary source of knowledge and wisdom about how to live a godly and righteous life.

Reading the Bible

As Christians, we believe that many of the moral and religious messages imbedded in biblical stories are universal, that they teach us about a God who operates at all times and in all places. Yet we often choose not to follow the literal messages in the Bible when they seem no longer relevant to our modern age. For instance, although most

Christians agree with the Old Testament injunction against murder, few pay attention to the ban against eating pork. Thus, we interpret the Bible selectively. Where appropriate, we use its words literally: "Love your neighbor as yourself [Matt. 19:19]" has remained a timeless statement. But when the Bible uses formulas no longer relevant for our lives, we reinterpret the words in sermons and in our own minds so that the same message comes through in a modern context. "You shall not covet your neighbor's . . . ox [Exod. 20:17]" is mentally translated quickly into "Do not covet your neighbor's expensive car."

Understanding what the Bible has to say about economic life may be particularly difficult for many modern readers. Unlike Abraham and Isaac, we no longer live in a tribal society. Unlike David or Amos, few of us are shepherds. Unlike Jesus and his disciples, we are not asked to obey the political dictates of the emperor of Rome. In fact, one reason that religion has become divorced from economic issues in our modern society may be that the direct economic messages that pervade the Bible appear to have little connection with the economic choices in our lives today.

It is not easy for most Americans to read passages that call them to forgive debts, to share property, or to give all their possessions to the poor. To discover the relevance of these passages in our lives we must interact with the text as we read it. As we listen to the biblical stories, we must constantly ask ourselves, "What does this mean about my behavior in my life today?" In some cases we may discover that these words, difficult as they are, have direct meaning for our lives. In other cases it may be necessary to translate the direct message in a way that preserves the underlying call for economic justice, but adjusts it to our current time and place.

Our own past history heavily influences this type of interactive reading and interpretation. We read through the lenses of our own experience. Those of us who are white, middle-income Americans tend to "see" the text in a way that is very different from the view of those who come from other cultural, economic, and racial backgrounds. For instance, those who have worked hard to achieve economic security respond very differently to the news that God feeds the hungry without charge and sends the rich away empty (Luke 1:53) than do those who are struggling with unemployment or discrimination. There is always a temptation to ignore or downplay the texts that make us uncomfortable and to concentrate on those that are most easily adaptable to our lives. It may be useful to read some of the more radical passages on economic life and to ask explicitly, "How would I interpret and 'see' this passage if I were unemployed and struggling to survive economically? If my great-grandfather had been born a slave? If my parents had fled political or economic oppression in another country?"

Selective interpretation of the biblical message is unavoidable. Even when we listen to a familiar biblical passage, such as the Twenty-third Psalm, we hear it differently in a time of deep grief than we do in a time of great joy. In part, this occurs because the Bible is a complex book with multiple levels of meaning. It also reflects the fact that we can see in the text only that which our own experience prepares us to understand. A person who has never felt deep grief may never recognize the depths of anger and pain in many of the psalms.

There is no single correct interpretation of the economic messages in the Bible. The Bible does not speak from a single voice. For instance, even when Luke tells the same stories as Mark, he often gives them a different emphasis or interpretation. And each reader will bring his or her own lenses to these stories. There are, however, some general themes about economic justice and economic decision making which recur throughout the biblical stories, in both the Old and New Testaments. Scholars have come to see these themes as crucial parts of the biblical message, not because of any specific passage that proves their importance, but because of their repetition throughout the Bible. The following sections outline three of these recurrent themes that speak directly to our economic lives.

Theme 1: A God Concerned with Economics

Throughout the Bible, God manifests a deep concern for economic justice and economic well-being among God's people. The theologian Douglas Meeks argues that one of God's primary roles in the Bible is to be an economist. God the Economist acts in history to assure that the household of God's people is a just household, where all have the resources necessary for life.

The formative event of the Old Testament is God's liberation of slaves from Egypt. Although this is a religious event, resulting in a covenant of faithfulness between God and the Chosen People, it is also a political and an economic event. God leads the Israelites out of the oppressive household of Pharaoh, out of slavery and into freedom, establishing a new household and a new economic system. God cares for the physical needs of the Israelites, providing manna in the desert. God gives the law, which not only teaches the proper forms of worship, but also sets out an economic and political framework for the Israelites to live by, designed to assure a just distribution of resources.

The Law of the Old Testament explicitly protects the rights of the least powerful and most needy in the household of the Israelites. These include the poor, the stranger, the sojourner, the widow, and the orphan. God's people are directed to tend to the needs of these most marginalized groups and to be sure that they receive their just share of the community's resources (Deuteronomy 10:17–18). There is to be a regular redistribution of property and the forgiveness of past debts (Leviticus 25:1–55; Deuteronomy 15:1–11). It is clear that God demands that a faithful people order both their spiritual and their material lives in ways that are pleasing to God.

This emphasis on economic and social justice as well as spiritual faithfulness recurs throughout the prophecies of the Old Testament. Isaiah speaks of economic prosperity and peace as an integral part of God's desire for Israel. Amos, Jeremiah, and Micah denounce the political and economic injustices within Israel, as well as its spiritual practices.

Jesus' ministry continues this theme. Jesus talks as much about economics in his teachings as he does about spiritual life. Many of the Gospel stories directly pose the question "What sort of economic decisions should one make to be faithful to God?" How should Nicodemus make retribution for his past life? Should Mary spend her time cooking or listening to Jesus speak? How should the wise steward use his master's money? What should the rich young man do with his possessions? What role should the money changers have in the church? These stories are both metaphors for spiritual lessons as well as direct lessons in economic decision making.

Jesus not only feeds the souls of his followers, but also literally feeds their bodies with loaves and fishes (Mark 6:35–44; Mark 8:1–10). Jesus emphasizes that the hungry shall be fed in God's realm (Luke 6:21) and feeding the hungry here on earth is a way to do God's will (Matthew 25:31–45). He castigates those who focus on material possessions as the primary aim in life and who do not share their wealth with others. His story contrasting the behavior of the rich with that of the widow who quietly gives from her meager resources to help the poor (Mark 12:41–44; Luke 21:1–4) remains a compelling indictment of the selfishness exhibited by those who have too much and give too little.

What emerges is a clear message that God is not only concerned with the spiritual life of God's followers, but that God also cares deeply about their economic life. Individual economic decisions, as well as the economic structures of the church and the government, are subject to God's judgment and God's demands.

Theme 2: God's Covenant with the Human Household

Closely connected to God's concern for the economic– and noneconomic–life of God's people, is the idea of a covenant between God and the people of God. Although the interpretation of this covenant changes through the Old and New Testaments, in all cases it is clear that the covenant involves mutual responsibilities on the part of both God and God's people.

The initial biblical covenant emerges at the beginning of Genesis, as a shared promise between Creator and creation. The Creator fills the world with good things, providing abundance and livelihood for all living creatures. The creation, both human and nonhuman, is charged with using this abundance in accord with the created order. Adam and Eve are driven out of Eden when they attempt to become something other than that which God intends, when their pride sets them against God. Human beings, made in the image of God, serve God by working as God's agents in the creation.

Some theologians have written about the Creation as a three-way covenant between God, humanity, and the nonhuman creation. In this view, humanity is not set over the rest of creation, but lives in harmony with creation; the earth provides abundance in exchange for humanity's care and nurture of the good things God has made. This interpretation of the creation has deep economic implications regarding appropriate human use of the environment.

The covenant between God and the Israelites becomes explicit under Moses' leadership. At this time, the Israelites are chosen to receive the law. In return, they pledge to worship God and to order their household in accordance with God's wishes. As we have seen, this includes explicit attention to the economic order by which they live.

Because of God's covenant, God remains faithful to the Israelites, acting in history to assure their survival. God also demands that they fulfill their covenantal responsibilities. The prophets are sent to call Israel back to faithfulness, both in spirit and in action. Again and again it is clear that faithfulness to God involves more than proper temple worship; the covenantal responsibilities of God's people encompass the entire range of their individual and community lives. God, speaking through Isaiah, describes the type of worship that brings the Lord's blessing: "If you offer your food to the hungry and satisfy the needs of the afflicted, then . . . the Lord will guide you continually [Isa. 8:10–11]."

In Jesus' ministry, God's promises are expanded beyond the tribe of Israel to a far more inclusive household. All willing followers are promised a part in this new covenant. Jesus offers God's mercy to all people, but also makes it clear that accepting God's offer means committing one's whole life to God. Jesus' followers are explicitly called to follow his example; to be God's agents in the world, healing the sick, caring for the poor, and challenging the powerful.

This theme of covenant illuminates the nature of human responsibilities in the light of God's concern for economic justice. As Christians who have accepted the promise of Jesus, we are brought into covenant with all peoples. God's household becomes our household, and there are no longer any strangers among us. Charged with carrying out God's will, we are called to see that all persons have the resources–spiritual and economic–necessary for life.

Theme 3: God's Special Concern for the Poor

Our covenant with God binds all of us within God's care and concern. Yet stories throughout the Bible emphasize that God has a particular concern for the poor and the oppressed. As people who seek to do God's will, we too are called to give special attention to the well-being of the poor.

The law received by Moses emphasizes the responsibilities of the Israelites to care for widows, orphans, and strangers, persons who would typically have no means of economic support (Exodus 22:22; Deuteronomy 10:18; Deuteronomy 15:7–11). Throughout the Old and New Testaments, the reader learns that certain persons are particularly good and righteous in stories that show them giving shelter to travelers or assistance to the poor. The parable of the good Samaritan (Luke 10:29–37) is probably the best known of these.

Jesus' own life, beginning in poverty and ending with death as a political prisoner, embodies God's particular concern for the poor. Through Jesus, God becomes one with the poor and lives in suffering love with their pain and oppression. In Luke, Jesus begins his ministry with the announcement that he has been appointed to preach the good news to the poor, to proclaim liberty to the captives, and to set at liberty the oppressed (Luke 4:18). The identification of God with the poor is nowhere better expressed than in Jesus' words, "Truly I tell you, just as you did it to one of the least of these who are members of my family, you did it to me [Matt. 25:40]."

The statement that God cares particularly for the poor is often heard as an exclusive statement. If God is particularly concerned for the poor, does this mean that God has less concern for the well-being of those who do not suffer daily hunger or oppression? To hear this as an exclusive statement is to ignore God's infinite capacity for love. Parents of a child who is experiencing difficult personal problems may feel a special concern for that child, but do not love or care for their other children any less. To proclaim God's concern for the poor in no way implies that God is not concerned for middle-income Christians as well. However, it does imply that middle-income Christians are called to share in God's concern.

The message that God cares particularly for the needs of the poor is linked with the message that those who are not poor have special responsibilities. Those with food are called to share it. Those with a home are called to provide a bed for the homeless. Those who sit in the councils of power are called to listen to the cries of the powerless. Those who have profited from injustice are called to repent and make restitution.

What Does This Mean About Our Faith?

These three biblical themes are by no means the only ones that link our faith with our economic lives, but they are a good starting point. From them emerge several important implications for the life of the church and for the life of individual Christians.

Christians are called to be fundamentally concerned about their neighbors, which means to be concerned with the household (economy) of God's people. Our covenantal responsibilities as Christians demand that we consider the well-being of all members of the human household in all our actions. We are to work toward the full inclusion of all our neighbors into one common household, assuring that everyone has access to the resources necessary for life and that everyone is allowed to participate fully in the life of the community. This is not a substitute for spiritual outreach, but a complement to it. We are called to both proclaim the presence of

God in our midst and to live a life that reveals that presence by fighting against poverty and oppression and striving for economic justice.

This emphasis on community, covenant, and shared responsibilities and obligations, may at times come into direct conflict with our modern lives. Messages from the contemporary world often encourage us to live for ourselves and to focus solely on our own or our family's needs. Although all of us have important responsibilities to our families and to ourselves that should not be taken lightly, the biblical vision calls us to a larger sense of who and what we are. We are not just individuals or small family groups, required to make only self-focused decisions. We are members of a community, who may be called to invest time and effort in responding to the needs of others.

Even when community concerns are explicitly recognized, it is often tempting to limit the definition of community. We are Americans, who live in a particular state, city, and neighborhood. Although these are important communities, the answer to "Who is my neighbor?" is broader than their boundaries. Our sense of "neighborness" is consistently being challenged and enlarged by our Christian commitments. Ultimately, our neighbors live around the globe.

Christians are called to recognize the interconnectedness of worship and just action. The biblical themes previously highlighted emphasize the inclusive nature of God's call. Biblical faithfulness involves more than regular and proper worship and daily prayer, although these are crucial parts of any Christian life. God is also worshiped by faithful daily living, which means dealing fairly and justly with all neighbors, whether they are nearby or far away. God judges both individuals and nations who are not faithful and who deal unjustly with the poor and powerless.

Nothing in our entire realm of daily living can be divorced from our religious life. Our lives demonstrate our Christian commitments in many ways, not least of which is to seek God's will in our personal economic decisions and to build and maintain social, economic, and political institutions that operate inclusively and justly.

Christians are called to listen to the voices of the poor and to seek reform and redress for injustices. God's particular concern for the poor must be mirrored by those who act as God's agents within the human household. On a personal level, Christians are regularly challenged to ask, "How much of my time and energy should I give to others?" Some of this giving will be directed to our extended family, our friends and co-workers, and our actual next-door neighbors. Listening to the trouble of a long-time friend is an important act of love. We must, however, also be available to listen to the needs and pain of those we may never meet face-to-face, whose lives may be very different from our own.

Jesus challenges the affluent to put on the "lenses" of the poor and to see how life looks to those who have less. He challenges the comfortable to view life through the eyes of those of a different race or different nationality. This means opening ourselves to the uncomfortable confession that our personal and institutional lifestyles sometimes contribute to the poverty, fear, and powerlessness of others. In our modern world, this is a challenge both to individual Christians and to the institutional church.

Summary

The Bible is a primary source of information about our faith. How we read it is heavily influenced by our own personal histories and experiences. It can be useful to recognize explicitly some of the biases that we bring to our own reading of the Bible, and to work at seeing biblical passages through alternative perspectives. There are a number of themes within the Bible that relate to economic issues. These include God's concern about the economic life of God's faithful people; the sense of covenant between God and creation, including the interconnecting responsibilities between those within God's household; and God's special concern for the needs of the poor and oppressed. These themes provide information on how we are called to live our spiritual as well as our economic lives. As members of a faithful community, we are called to be God's agents in this world. This call means acting justly to all our neighbors, not only through our own personal behavior, but also through the institutions and structures that we create and maintain in order to live together in society.

GROUP DISCUSSION AND ACTIVITIES
Suggested Group Exercise

Divide the group in half. Designate one group as "poor." Have each individual imagine a role for him- or herself that matches this designation (a recent immigrant, a inner-city African American, a teenage mother, an elderly person with limited income, and so forth.) Designate the other group as "well-off" and ask each person to imagine his or her role (a self-made business person, a successful doctor, a member of an affluent family, a person who has inherited substantial income, and so on). Tell the members of this subgroup that they are all faithful churchgoers. Ask each group to read and discuss the following four passages within their respective roles: Deuteronomy 15:1–11, Mark 12:14–17, Luke 6:20–25, and Luke 18:22–25. As each group discusses these passages, it should decide what it wants to tell the other group about the faith lessons that should be drawn from these passages.

Bring both groups together. Give members of each group a chance to tell members of the other what they heard in these passages about their faith. Then, give each group a chance to respond and to discuss the different perspectives.

Starting Discussion Questions

1. Give examples from the Bible in which God acts as an economist. How do you respond to this image to God?

2. How do you respond to the claim that God has a special concern for the poor and the oppressed? What might this mean?

3. Read the discussion of the Sabbatical Year and the Jubilee Year in Leviticus 25. Is there any way to translate these requirements into those that might make sense in today's world? What are the underlying themes in this chapter? What are the underlying behavioral principles that God is trying to reinforce through these laws?

CHAPTER 3

Human Suffering in Today's Household

When the United Church of Christ asked a group of us to write a statement on the linkages between theology and economic justice, we quickly discovered that we were in fundamental disagreement over how to begin talking about the theological issues. One group insisted that the committee should start with the question "What does the Bible tell us about economic justice and injustice?" The other group insisted that the committee should start with the question "How do we experience injustice in our own lives?" The first group wanted to begin with a biblically based exploration of the theological issues, whereas the second group wanted to start with life experiences.

Perhaps it is not surprising that it was the African American, Asian American and Hispanic members of the committee who felt most strongly that it was important to begin by telling the *stories* of injustice. For them, it was their own recurring personal experiences with injustice that most motivated their religious concern about this issue.

There is no need to choose between these two approaches. On the one hand, we can affirm the concern for justice and peace that emerges from biblical investigation; on the other hand, we can intensify our personal concern with these issues by learning the stories of poverty and injustice told by our neighbors in today's world. Thus this chapter, although very different from the previous chapter that explored biblical backgrounds, is also fundamentally a theological chapter that explores the nature of human sin.

Poverty in the Midst of Affluence

The average American family in 1990 had $35,700 to live on, according to official income statistics of the United

States. While far from classifying its recipients as rich, such income is beyond the wildest dreams of many in our country and elsewhere in the world, as it would have been beyond the dreams of many of our parents and grandparents. Of course, this overall average ignores the enormous variation among different types of families. Women with children who head their own households had an average income of only $18,000. In contrast, households whose primary wage earner had completed college had average incomes of $50,500.

Ironically, for many whose income is well above average, surviving on the typical family's $36,000 a year would appear an almost impossible hardship. Families with higher incomes commit themselves to homes and lifestyles that require more money. Thus, even those who are relatively wealthy in the United States often feel pressed by economic need. Very few Americans consider themselves rich. Compared with those who are truly poor in America, however, most Americans are indeed well off.

The United States defines an official "poverty line," the income level below which a person or family is considered poor. To be counted as poor in America (according to 1990 statistics), two parents and two children must live on less than $13,360; a mother and a child are considered poor if their income is below $8790; a single elderly person is counted as poor if his or her income is below $6270. In most communities in the United States today, it is virtually impossible to find decent housing and have enough money left over for other necessities at these income levels. As a result, poor families typically move in with other relatives (often only a short-term possibility), live in overcrowded or substandard housing, and move frequently in search of a better or more affordable home.

In 1990, 33.6 million Americans were considered poor. This is 13.5 percent of the entire U.S. population and is equivalent to the combined populations of Indiana, Illinois, Michigan, and Wisconsin. Of course, poverty is not spread evenly across the population. Some groups are far more likely than others to be poor.

Women with children who head their own households are the most likely to be poor in this country. Forty-four percent of all female-headed families live below the poverty line. Among African American and Hispanic women, half are poor, and high levels of poverty among women are strongly correlated with poverty among children. Child poverty rates in the United States were higher in the late 1980s than they had been for two decades: In 1990, for example, more than one child in five lived in a poor household. Among children who live only with their mothers, the poverty rates are shockingly high: two-thirds of African American and Hispanic children who live only with their mothers are poor, and more than 50 percent of all white children who live only with their mothers are poor. In a land concerned with the opportunities available to its youngest members, such numbers are chilling.

Hand-in-hand with poverty go problems of health. A major indicator of progress against poverty is the infant mortality rate of a country. Of the almost 4 million babies born in the United States annually, close to 40,000 will not survive their first year. The United States ranks twenty-second in infant mortality among industrialized nations; in Japan and the Scandinavian countries, infant death rates are half that of the United States. Infant mortality rates among African American infants are particularly high–as high as in nonindustrial countries such as Costa Rica.

Even among the poor, there are gradations of need. At the extreme edge of survival are the homeless. Since the early 1980s, the visibility of homelessness in cities across America has been growing. Largely because of changing land values in urban areas, the availability of very low rent apartments or rooms have sharply decreased. This situation has displaced people, who are then unable to find alternative affordable housing. The homeless are a very mixed group. Between one third to one half are persons who have some history of treatment for mental disabilities. However, one fourth to one third of the homeless population are mothers and children. Many others are single men between the ages of twenty and fifty, who have lost their access to the cheap single rooms where they once lived.

The problem of poverty in the United States is not unrelievedly bleak. Many persons believe the myth that the War on Poverty launched in the 1960s was a total failure.

While serious poverty problems continue in this country, we have been able to reduce need among some groups, indicating that public policy efforts against poverty can be effective. For instance, an enormous expansion in government assistance programs for elderly Americans in the 1960s and 1970s has produced striking reductions in poverty among the elderly. Individuals over age sixty-five in this country are now less likely to be poor than those under age sixty-five. Many have pointed to the general situation of the elderly as evidence that expanded public assistance programs can substantially decrease economic need. In addition, a major expansion has occurred over the past two decades in the availability of public health insurance (Medicaid) to the poorest families in the United States. A wide variety of studies have credited this program with improving the health of its recipients. Although there are many not covered by Medicaid—over 30 million low-income persons currently have no health insurance and even some on Medicaid have difficulty finding available health care—Medicaid has been expanded in recent years to cover all young children in poor and near-poor families. In addition, a vast expansion of the food stamp program occurred in the early to mid-1970s, providing coupons to low-income families that can be exchanged for food in most grocery stores. Although food stamps have not eliminated hunger in America, they have substantially reduced the occurrence of serious malnutrition and malnutrition-related diseases.

Any discussion of poverty in the United States must be a story with both good news and bad news: The good news is that concerted public efforts to improve the lives of poor people have had positive results. But the bad news is that problems of poverty in this country are far from solved. Too many of our neighbors are struggling daily with inadequate housing, poor health, and insufficient income. The U.S. Catholic Bishops, in their recent letter on economic justice, said it as bluntly as anyone: "That so many people are poor in a nation as rich as ours is a social and moral scandal that we cannot ignore."

Discrimination and Economic Exclusion

Poverty does not occur randomly. There are reasons why some groups are disproportionately poor and other groups are disproportionately well-off. Discrimination in jobs, education, and economic opportunities has affected members of racial and ethnic minorities, women, older workers, and persons of different sexual orientation, among others.

Racism in America may be the most pervasive and destructive social problem that this society has faced and still faces. The human slavery of the early decades of this country's history evolved into a form of economic slavery in the years following the Civil War, when African Americans were given little chance of economic advancement and no political voice. The civil rights movement of the 1960s brought enormous political and economic change for African Americans, including vastly expanded access to educational institutions, a changing mix of job opportunities, new avenues of political participation, and the growth of a middle-class African American population. Yet at the beginning of the 1990s, this progress remains strikingly incomplete.

Poverty rates among African Americans are three times higher than among white Americans; unemployment rates are close to twice as high. Even among the nonpoor, African American families earn less, have less wealth, receive less education, and have poorer health. Although wage rates among African American men steadily increased relative to white men for almost two decades, since 1980 this progress has stopped and even gone backward slightly. Recent layoffs and loss of jobs in the U.S. manufacturing sector, which has historically employed a disproportionately large share of African Americans, have hit African American families particularly hard. African American men who work full time earn less than three fourths of that earned by white men.

Despite long-term efforts at housing integration, a substantial portion of the African American community remains in very poor, segregated inner city communities. Nearby job opportunities in many of these areas have declined steadily. Growing problems of crime and drugs in these communities have created victims among innocent bystanders, as well as young men who are recruited at an early age into a web of violence and crime. The full set of reasons behind these problems are too many and too complex to describe here in any detail. Obviously, there is an explosive social situation when one group with seemingly few personal opportunities lives in the midst of an affluent society.

Even among middle-income persons, there is still often a wariness across racial lines. A rising number of hostile racial incidents have occurred on the streets and campuses of this country. Efforts to rescind civil rights legislation at the national level give African Americans the sense that their progress is still tenuous. African American professionals tell painful stories of being excluded from the social networks of their offices or treated with uncomfortable unease. In the words of the recent Committee on the Status of Black Americans, "The status of black Americans today can be characterized as a glass that is half full—if measured by progress since 1939—or as a glass that is half empty—if measured by the persisting disparities between black and white Americans since the early 1970s."

While black-white racial strife holds a unique place in American history, the growing Hispanic population in this country faces similar problems, exemplified by extreme poverty, and often exacerbated by language difficulties. In many southwestern states, Hispanics are the dominant minority group; if current growth trends continue, the Hispanic population will surpass the African American population by early in the next century. Hispanics as a group are very heterogeneous, ranging from Puerto Ricans to Mexican Americans to Salvadorans and Cubans. Each of these groups has come to the United States out of a different political and cultural history and faces a different set of problems and issues. Increasing political and social attention in the years ahead will surely focus on efforts by Hispanic Americans to move toward greater economic security and political participation.

Other groups have also felt the destructive anger of society directed toward their "differentness." Only in recent years has this country begun to confess its sin when, during World War II, it seized the property of West Coast Japanese Americans and interned them. And the group with the claim to the most sustained injustice in this country is the Native American population that lived here long before European settlers arrived. Although there are no official poverty rates published regularly for Native Americans, evidence indicates that this group is probably poorer than any other. Large numbers of Native Americans live on reservation land, with few job opportunities.

The problems of exclusion and discrimination experienced by women in the economy are not quite the same as those faced by racial and ethnic minorities. Men and women live and work together daily, but the pain of economic exclusion that results because of biased stereotypes about women's roles and abilities is very real. Low wages among women are often the result of the type of jobs that women are hired to do. Sexual segregation within jobs is much more common than racial segregation. Many "women's jobs" require interpersonal and/or educational skills, but pay very low wages. High rates of poverty among women who head families are partly a result of their limited job opportunities.

Such poverty is also the result of social inequities in terms of who bears economic responsibility for children. Among women raising children on their own, only about half have any sort of award of child support from the absent father, and only half of women with such awards regularly receive the full amount. As a result, the average child support payment received by a woman living on her own with her children is around $1000 per year. With the burden of combined responsibilities for child care and for income earning, it is hardly surprising that many women end up in poverty.

Economic exclusion comes in many forms. It starts when the public schools in some areas are poorly staffed and funded, or when girls are encouraged to avoid math and science courses. It continues when jobs are not available near segregated housing areas, or when employers are willing to hire certain groups of workers only into low-skill, dead-end jobs. It continues as workers of a different ethnicity, race, or gender are treated differently on the job.

Economic Dislocation

In the midst of a changing economy, all workers are at risk of losing their jobs. Company reorganization or the adoption of new technologies may mean new opportunities for some, but often means unemployment for others. In times of recession, the threat of unemployment is even greater. Between June 1990 and June 1991, over 2 million people lost their jobs because of economic recession.

During the last decade in the United States there have been major shifts in the economy. Because of increasing international competition, the manufacturing sector has been particularly hard hit. Employment in manufacturing has declined steadily, with particularly great losses in the number of high-wage jobs for skilled manufacturing labor. For many decades, a high school degree and a willingness to work was, in most industrial communities, enough to assure an individual of a good job with good wages. Many of these communities have come to realize this is no longer true. Younger workers are unable to find jobs that promise the secure and steady wages their parents received. Between 1979 and 1987, earnings of high school graduates between the ages of 25 and 34 fell by over 11 percent (adjusting for inflation).

Many of those disemployed in manufacturing have found jobs in the expanding service sector. Many service sector jobs pay well; areas such as health and financial services have experienced expanded employment and rising wages. Most well-paying jobs, however, require educational credentials beyond high school. Young men with only a high school degree receive $4000 less in service jobs than do similar workers in manufacturing jobs.

As a result of these changes and others, there has been a steady widening in the wage distribution among American workers. Workers with college degrees experienced substantial wage growth in the 1980s, but workers with less schooling experienced substantial wage declines in the same period. Economic dislocation does not occur only with unemployment. It can also happen when a family works hard and finds itself losing ground, which has been the experience of many workers during the past decade.

Farmers are another group that experienced serious economic problems during the 1980s. Family farmers have faced particularly severe problems in some areas of the country, and the rate of farm foreclosure has increased. Newspapers around the country have carried many moving stories about families forced to sell farms worked by several generations.

No modern economic system has been successful in preventing unemployment or worker relocation. One reason is that business and government economic policies are too little concerned with the costs of unemployment among workers. Another is that changing technologies and shifting consumer demands necessarily lead to expansion in some firms and contraction in others. In a changing society, some economic disruption is inevitable and even desirable. The question we face as a society is how to deal with the effects of such change. For instance, plant shutdowns that occur without notice can devastate a community and its workers. Laws requiring firms to give workers early warning of potential problems sometimes allow firms, workers, and the surrounding community to work together to prevent a shutdown, as experience with such laws in states such as Maine has indicated. When shutdowns are inevitable, assistance in transition planning for the community and job search and retraining for the workers can significantly reduce the costs of plant closure.

Poverty and Economic Dislocation on a Global Level

Although poverty and economic pain among our own American citizens may be immediately visible to most of us, global problems of malnutrition, disease, illiteracy, and political and economic oppression are far greater. Income levels that mean poverty in the United States may mean wealth in many other countries.

The incidence of poverty and need among the world's people is stunningly high. The World Bank estimates that 1.1 billion people in developing countries are poor, where poverty is defined as having an income of about $1.00 per day. There are 630 million people considered by the World Bank to be in "extreme poverty," facing daily problems of disease, malnutrition, and contaminated water. Bread for the World estimates that 500 million persons are hungry on a daily basis. Each day, 40,000 children die from disease and malnutrition, causes that are, in most cases, completely preventable.

One of the tragic aspects of the world hunger problem is that it is not caused by an overall world shortage of food. The problem is not too many mouths and too little food, but is instead the *distribution* of food resources. Only a very few countries actually lack the land or other resources to grow enough food for adequate nutrition among their population. However, local agriculture is often disrupted by war or political problems, or by land ownership patterns that result in large amounts of agricultural land set aside to produce crops for export rather than for domestic consumption. For instance, in Guatemala hunger increased when small farmers were forced off their land, which had provided food to their families, and large farms were created to produce crops sold for cash to large corporations. Although the sale of export crops made more money on this land than the small farmers had been able to realize, very little of that income came back to the displaced families and they were left poorer and hungrier.

Wars between and within countries are also a major cause of hunger and economic dislocation. Cambodia, long the breadbasket of Southeast Asia, experienced several years of devastating famine in the late 1970s because of a vicious government regime that completely disrupted the agriculture of the country and terrorized its people. Villagers were killed or forced to move, spring planting was disrupted, and, in the midst of a rich and fertile environment, a million Cambodians died of hunger, almost one fifth of the population. Similarly, the ongoing famines in the Sudan and in Ethiopia are the result of a number of dry years, which by themselves would have caused serious agricultural problems, combined with internal fighting between rival tribal groups that has displaced whole populations from their villages and their sources of income.

Poverty is closely linked with health problems. The most notable achievement in global health care in the past decade has been the complete eradication of smallpox. Still, thousands of deaths from disease and infection occur daily, which could be readily prevented by the availability of uncontaminated water and basic medical care. For instance, the World Bank estimates that 30 million children under age five in developing countries die each year of illnesses that would not usually be fatal in industrialized countries.

Closely linked to problems of poverty and economic disruption is the pain experienced by the tens of thousands of refugees who are displaced each year. The number of refugees—persons who have been forced to leave their homes because of persecution, war, or natural disaster—has grown substantially over the past decade to more than 12 million persons. The loss of home is made worse for many of these families by the hostile treatment they receive when they cross borders to a new community or country, where they are often considered both an economic burden and a political threat. In some cases, as in the situation of the Palestinians, several generations of families have grown up in crowded and "temporary" refugee camps.

The level of global economic need is so great as to be entirely overwhelming. It is impossible to comprehend the meaning of 500 million hungry people, much less to find ways to respond. No one person can substantially relieve global hunger, but any individual can work to make a difference in a few lives. Although many of these global problems might seem far away, virtually all Americans have some connection to the national economies of a wide variety of other nations. From coffee to chocolate and from shirts to shoes, the products we buy in our local stores often come from countries throughout the world, traded by corporations for whom we work and from whom we buy. Like others in the developed world, our lives and our

economic decisions are intimately connected with the lives
and well-being of farmers and workers around the world.

Militarization

War is a major cause of economic need and injustice on
virtually every continent. Almost 130 wars have been fought
around the globe *since* World War II. When war comes to a
land, families are forced out of their homes, lose their
livelihoods, and face the death or disappearance of parents,
spouses, and children. Many of those who have lived in fear
of death, torture, or imprisonment can never feel entirely
secure again.

Although the destruction of war is most devastating,
preparation for war and military buildup designed to prevent war can also have high costs. The United States, which
has not seen actual combat on its own continental territory
since the Civil War, has still been deeply affected by war
and preparation for war. Every dollar spent for military-
related purposes is a dollar not spent for other purposes.
The steady rise in defense spending in the early 1980s
resulted in a $300 billion military budget by 1990. To un-
derstand the size of this budget, realize that this is the
equivalent of spending $285 *every minute* since Jesus's birth.
By 1988 (adjusting for the effects of inflation) the United
States was spending as much on the military as it had at the
height of the Vietnam War twenty years earlier.

This buildup in military spending in the 1980s had at
least two effects. First, because there are always limited
government resources, social domestic programs were cut
during this period. Between 1981 and 1985, when military
spending increased by 70 percent, spending on education
increased only 6 percent and spending on job training declined by 70 percent. The high rates of child poverty we
face today are at least partially linked to these changes in
public spending.

Second, such spending was highly focused on the design
and production of a variety of large weapons systems, requiring extensive scientific and technical expertise. The
demand by the military for mathematicians, computer pro-

grammers, engineers, and physicists grew in these years, raising their wages and increasing the share of these workers employed in military-related projects. Thus it was harder for educational institutions to hire such people for teaching positions. It was also more difficult for firms producing consumer products to hire top-quality research and design personnel. Some analysts have indicated that part of the market loss in electronic products that occurred for U.S. companies in the 1980s was related to the fact that many of our best scientific personnel were drawn into military rather than civilian-related research.

At a global level, the diversion of resources into military spending is enormous. Over $850 trillion were spent on military weapons and personnel by all governments combined in 1986, approximately 5.6 percent of total world income. In contrast, only 4.9 percent of world income was spent on education and only 4.1 percent on health.

It is particularly troubling that the amount of money spent on arms and military personnel is increasing more rapidly in poor countries than in rich countries. In 1960, the military expenditures of the developing world were only 8 percent of those of the industrialized countries. By 1986, they were 41 percent. Such spending directly robs the poor, the ill, and the uneducated and makes the world less safe and a more threatening place for all of us.

Environmental Degradation

Intimately linked to our enduring ability to live peacefully with each other and to provide adequate food to all human beings, is our ability to preserve the beauty and abundance of creation. The last decade has witnessed a sharp rise in concern about the long-term effects of our economic systems on the health of this planet.

Clean air and clean water are necessary for health and life. In the United States, environmental regulations passed in the 1960s have produced substantial improvements in the air and water of many areas of the country, although significant problems continue to exist. Globally, many countries are only now beginning to realize the extent of their pollution problems. For instance, because of many years of unchecked industrial pollution in some countries in eastern Europe, there are towns where residents accept yellow skies and sooty, smelly air as normal.

Safe disposal of hazardous wastes from industrial production processes is another crucial economic problem. The U.S. government now has over 1200 hazardous waste contamination sites on its National Priorities List that pose health risks to families who live and work nearby. The cost of cleaning up waste dumps years after their creation is enormous; such dumps must be prevented from being created and abandoned.

Recent years of abnormally high temperatures around the globe have raised international concern about global warming. Measured globally, 1990 was the warmest year on record. The rising level of carbon dioxide and pollutants in the atmosphere, combined with depletion of ozone levels, may be creating an atmospheric change that could cause major ecological disruptions. Even a small long-term temperature change in the earth's atmosphere could disrupt agricultural growth patterns around the world.

Perhaps more than any other issue, environmental problems reveal the interconnectedness of nations. Pollution problems do not respect national boundaries, and the cost of pollution to a neighboring country may be as great as to the country in which it occurs.

Powerlessness and Exclusion

Many of those who suffer most have little opportunity to participate in the economic and political decision making of their society. Those who are poor frequently have little control over the forces that shape their lives. Lack of education, lack of health, or lack of a job can marginalize an individual in society and limit his or her life choices. Similarly, an oppressive political or an economic system, in which decisions are made by only a few persons, leaves powerless those who are excluded from leadership.

Even among middle-income Americans, with a well-guarded right to express their opinions and participate politically, there is often a sense of powerlessness. Unemployed steel workers in the Midwest were impacted by changes in international competition far beyond their own control. Mothers whose food stamps were cut in the early 1980s because of federal legislative changes had no involvement in that decision.

Thus, a fight for economic justice must often involve a fight for inclusive participation in the economic and social decisions that affect people's lives. Workplace organizations, such as unions or workers' councils, can provide one way for workers to be part of the economic decisions that affect them. Democratic political systems enfranchise people in similar ways. While any political system can become corrupt and exclusionary, it is only through building participatory social and economic institutions that the voices of all members of the community will have a chance of being heard.

Fear and the Distortion of Human Values

Economic injustices are often closely linked to fear: fear of economic insecurity, fear of poverty, and fear of the loss of power by those who currently hold power. Much of the ambivalence demonstrated by Americans toward issues of global poverty stems from such fear. Although most Americans are deeply moved by the images of starving children elsewhere in the world, their response is also affected by a fear that international needs are so great that they can be fully alleviated only by impoverishing wealthier nations. There is a deep fear of change in all of us, particularly if change means giving up that which we now have. Much of this fear is rooted in our own personal histories. Those of us who are secure today typically fear how easily that security can be lost, those who are struggling fear that change will make things worse, not better.

Some of these fears are realistic. Efforts to improve the wages and working conditions of persons in developing countries will translate directly into higher prices for the goods that they produce and we buy. However, fear too often exaggerates danger and ignores the positive results of change. If higher taxes today produce better public schools, we can all benefit from a more highly skilled work force tomorrow.

Greed, materialism, and selfishness are all human traits that can emerge when we fear losing that which we now have. Those who are among the "rich" of the world–which means most Americans–must fight against a distortion of values that places things above people. In a world of great inequality, both those who are poor and those who are rich are at risk of becoming spiritually impoverished. The poor suffer the assault of powerlessness and exclusion that can decrease their sense of their own humanity. The rich become enmeshed in a system that equates human worth with material possessions, distorting *their* sense of humanity.

Economic Injustice and Economic Pain

This chapter has discussed many types of economic pain, much of which evolves out of explicit economic injustices. It is important, however, to note that *change* in our modern economy is inevitable. And change inevitably brings loss. Most blacksmiths, for example, saw their skills become obsolete and lost their jobs forever. Yet change also brings new economic opportunities. Hundreds of thousands of persons now work as computer technicians, an occupation that did not exist twenty years ago.

Not all losses are preventable and not all economic pain is the result of injustice. Just as there remain diseases for which a cure remains elusive, so economic cycles and economic change necessarily will continue to produce economic pain. Injustice occurs when pain that is preventable is not prevented. In the today's world, there is no need for children to die of dehydration caused by diarrhea that results from foul water. But many do. In a country with the wealth of the United States, there is no need for hundreds of thousands to be homelessness in our urban areas. But they are.

Not all economic pain cannot be prevented, but individuals and nations can work to limit the extent of poverty, exclusion, and oppression. Sometimes this may mean avoiding decisions that cause pain. More often, it may mean making difficult decisions, at the same time trying to alleviate the pain that some will experience, such as assisting unemployed workers to relocate or train for other jobs.

Summary

The human suffering of those around us evokes a compassionate response. By listening to the stories of poverty and exclusion told by our neighbors, we can learn about injustice and human sin. These stories include tales of poverty and homelessness in the United States, as well as racial and ethnic discrimination. They also include the tales of unemployment and loss of community suffered by those in the midst of economic dislocation. At a global level, these stories are even more painful; they speak of famine, disease, and war. Military spending increases the diversion of resources away from human needs around the globe. Environmental degradation and pollution threaten the end of an abundant creation. All of these problems are intimately connected to the exclusion of many in the decisions that affect their lives. Powerlessness prevents change and stops persons from fighting against injustice. Similarly, overabundance and fear of loss can distort the values of those who have possessions and blind them to injustices around them.

GROUP DISCUSSION AND ACTIVITIES

Suggested Group Exercise

The average public assistance available to a woman with two children and no private sources of income in 1991 was $629 a month ($367 in welfare payments from Aid to Families with Dependent Children and $262 in food stamps) or $7548 a year. Discuss what a monthly budget would be for this woman in your community. (Note: Welfare payments from the Aid to Families with Dependent Children program will differ across states. If you can, find out the level for your state and use it.)

Starting Discussion Questions and Activities

1. Invite one of your church members or a local community member to talk about his or her own personal experiences with exclusion and/or racism. For example, the person could be a Japanese American whose family was interned during World War II, an African American, or a woman who works in a predominantly male occupation.

2. In what ways have you experienced economic pain? In what ways have you experienced economic injustice? How do these differ? When are they the same?

3. When you see newspaper or TV pictures of starving children in distant lands, such as Ethiopia, what are your reactions? Would you respond differently if they were children from your own community? How do you react to pictures of war? Do you respond differently if they involve U.S. troops?

CHAPTER 4

What Do We Seek?
Marks of a Just Economy

How do we order our economy so that all persons have the economic resources necessary to participate fully in society? In order to "do justice" we must have a framework by which to judge what is just and right action. This chapter helps define our economic responsibilities in God's household more clearly, by addressing the question "What does economic justice require?"

Good intentions alone are rarely enough to assure good actions. Individually and corporately, we have all committed blunders when we meant to do well. For instance, several years ago my local church decided to sponsor a refugee family from southeast Asia, helping them find housing and employment. One of our church volunteers went with the man of the family to verify the family's immigration status at the local Immigration and Naturalization Service office. Because his English was limited, she tried to help with the conversation. She and the INS official began to converse about the man's problems, too fast for him to understand, until he gently pushed her aside and explained, "I talk for me." It was a situation in which doing something for the man was not the help he needed; he needed someone to help him learn how to handle the situation by himself.

To avoid letting our good intentions lead us toward inappropriate action, it can be useful to develop standards by which to judge action. The group that worked together on the United Church of Christ *Pronouncement* developed ten such standards, which they called the "Marks of a Just Economy." These standards are designed to give definition to the biblical and theological call to be actively concerned with economic justice. They are grounded in some of the broad biblical themes noted in chapter 2 and also reflect the concerns in chapter 3 that emerge from our modern economic history. Thus, they serve as a bridge between biblical teaching and modern times.

Although these standards are stated as the requirements by which a larger economy can be judged just or unjust, they may operate just as well in guiding the behavior of an individual, a church, or a community. In our life together–our own behavior, as well as the behavior of the institutions that we create and in which we participate–our efforts can be held accountable to the following standards of economic justice.

Marks of a Just Economy

1. A just economy celebrates and serves the fundamental covenant purpose of human life, which is to love God and neighbor.

By calling ourselves Christian we evoke our faithfulness to the covenant symbolized in Jesus' life, death, and resurrection. This covenant calls all humanity into community together, affirms our mutual responsibilities to each other, and commits us to faithfulness to God. Our economic life must recognize this common humanity, providing opportunities to serve God and to serve other human beings. An economy violates this standard when it encourages its members to worship and to serve idols, such as material accumulation, military power, or the personality cults of its leaders.

2. A just economy gives all persons access to the basic material necessities of life.

Our common human responsibilities are violated when some members of the human community are excluded from the abundance of creation and do not have access to the resources necessary for life. Both in public and more privately with his disciples, Jesus shares bread as the fundamental symbol and affirmation of God's concern for the well-being of each person. In turn, we are instructed to share bread with our brothers and sisters everywhere. Injustice occurs whenever there is starvation, homelessness, or poverty.

3. A just economy builds and enhances human communities of dignity and well-being.

The emphasis of our faith is on *community*. Even the worship of God is defined as a community activity. ("Where two or three are gathered in my name, I am there among them [Matt. 18:20].") To be a whole individual one cannot be isolated, but must be part of a larger community. This is also true of our economic life. We cannot live independently, but depend on the talents and work of all those around us, so that all of our needs might be met. A just economy strengthens human community, emphasizing the interconnectedness of needs and responsibilities that exist between people. An economy violates this standard when it encourages individuals to place their own personal advancement over all other goals.

4. A just economy is inclusive, involving all able people in responsible, participatory, and economically rewarding activity.

Our covenant with God is one of mutual responsibilities: God promises God's ongoing presence and mercy, and individuals promise to worship God and seek to act in accord with God's will. Similarly, the covenant between individuals in an economy is also one of mutual responsibilities. All individuals are invited into full participation in the life of the community. This means first that all able persons are expected to engage in productive work that benefits the larger economy. Second, it means that all members of a community are enabled and expected to participate in shared decision making. In return, the larger community has a responsibility to assure that each individual has access to job opportunities that pay a fair return for labor. Economic injustice occurs when productive members of an economy seek work but cannot find it, or when persons work at steady, full-time jobs but earn too little to purchase adequate food and housing.

5. A just economy encourages creativity, skill, and diligence.

A just economy does not expect that all persons are identical. Rather it recognizes the multiplicity of talents among all human beings, and encourages each individual to pursue his or her own skills and creative abilities. Economic institutions that encourage personal choice, reward persistence, and stimulate creativity allow each person a chance to contribute most effectively to the economy. This enhances the personal worth and dignity of individuals and expands the productivity of society. Injustice occurs when children grow up with no sense of opportunity or choice about their future, or when employees are treated as machines rather than human beings.

6. A just economy assures equality of opportunity.

When every person is recognized as a full member of the household, then the community has the responsibility to provide each individual with a full set of opportunities. Race, sex, age, sexual orientation, or ethnic background should not determine access to education, jobs, health care, or political participation. Injustice occurs when economic opportunity is limited by group stereotypes.

7. A just economy reflects God's passion for the poor and disadvantaged, enhancing the life opportunities of the poor, the weak, and groups at the margin of society.

God's particular concern for the poor creates a responsibility within our human communities to given priority to those who are most in need. It is valid to ask of each economic decision, "How will this affect the poor among us?" Giving precedence to the needs of the poor does not mean just "doing for" the poor. It also means enabling them to speak for themselves, opening up decision-making forums to those who have been voiceless. This standard is violated when decision makers select economic policies that impose greater costs on the poor than on middle- or upper-income groups.

8. A just economy recognizes the integrity, fullness, and sacredness of creation.

Faithfulness to God demands faithfulness to God's creation. To meet the basic economic needs of all persons, we must rely on the abundance and bounty of the world in which we live. If we mistreat the environment, we mistreat

God's creation and will ultimately destroy ourselves. The economic production that supports human life is only one part of a larger created order. Economic decisions should not treat nature as subservient to human needs, but should respect the interconnected web of life within the creation. This standard is violated when economic decisions are made without regard to their environmental costs.

9. A just economy acknowledges the dignity of human beings as made known in Jesus Christ, and guarantees the basic human rights necessary to maintain the sacredness of individuals.

Human life is sacred to Christians. We are instructed not to kill, to refrain from harming our brothers and sisters, and to practice forgiveness. On the one hand, this means providing the economic resources necessary for life. Access to food and water are basic human rights. On the other hand, food alone is not all that is necessary for a person to be truly human. Political oppression also destroys human dignity. The government and legal structure of a community should assure that everyone can participate openly in its decisions. An economy is unjust when it supports a political regime that violates the rights of individuals to voice their opinion, to be free of unjust imprisonment, or to worship God in their own way.

10. A just economy requires and promotes international peace and well-being.

Peace and justice are inextricably linked. The absence of war does not mean peace if people are oppressed. Similarly, justice cannot exist in the midst of war, particularly modern war where civilians and combatants alike are always threatened by bombs. A commitment to a just peace means seeking peaceful ways to enact justice, and just structures to enforce peace. An economy that expends its resources on war or on armaments deprives others of life and deprives its own people of resources for food and health and education. Although there are times when some groups will feel impelled toward violent action, a just economy will encourage the use of nonviolent methods to deal with the inevitable conflicts and disagreements that arise between peoples. Injustice occurs when a nation seeks war as a solution to problems that may be settled by negotiation, sanctions, or third-party mediation.

What Do These Marks Mean?

It is never easy to translate general principles into specific criteria for action. Almost inevitably, the results will necessarily reflect the particular concerns of the translators. For instance, these particular standards for justice were written by a group of American citizens and were heavily shaped by the democratic political heritage they share. Some readers may disagree with one or more of these particular standards. Some may wish to add others to the list. There is no such thing as a complete or perfect list of standards by which to define justice.

These ten standards, however, provide a starting point by which we can evaluate and judge the economy in which we live, as well as any proposals for change. We can explicitly ask, "In what ways does our economy meet some of these criteria, and where does it fail?"

It is important to note that these ten marks of a just economy provide a purposefully utopian vision of justice. No humanly created economy will ever be fully inclusive and just for all people. This does not mean that such standards are useless or irrelevant. These ten standards of justice play a role similar to that of Isaiah's prophecies of peace and plenty. They provide a sense of the direction in which we want to move and a promise of what can be gained by going in that direction. This is a familiar situation for Christians: we live continuously in expectation of a new and better world, even as we seek to live faithfully in this present and imperfect world.

Summary

This chapter builds on the past two chapters to present a set of ten marks of a just economy. These standards describe an inclusive economy that provides the resources necessary for full and productive life to all individuals, strengthening their ties to each other and promoting a peaceful and productive society. These ten standards provide a set of criteria against which we can judge our current economic communities and present the vision and promise of what it is we seek.

GROUP DISCUSSION AND ACTIVITIES

Suggested Group Exercise

Divide participants into five or ten small groups. Assign each group one or two of the "Marks of a Just Economy." Ask group members to discuss the meaning of these standards and provide several examples from the economies with which they are familiar (their families, their workplaces, the local community, the nation) where this aspect of justice is present, and several examples in which this aspect of justice is denied. Call participants together to describe and discuss these examples in the larger group.

Starting Discussion Questions

1. Are there criteria for economic justice that you believe are missing from this list? Are there criteria here that you disagree with?

2. Indicate other attempts in our religious heritage to develop guidelines that translate theological principles into criteria for action. (Example: The Ten Commandments might be considered "marks of just Christian living.") Have there been similar attempts in our political heritage to translate political principles into guidelines for action?

CHAPTER 5
Understanding Our Market Economy

The last four chapters developed a faith-based perspective on economics and economic justice. This chapter and the next, changing the focus entirely, look at our modern economy and how it works. If the last few chapters were written from a theological perspective, then these next two are written from an economist's perspective. This chapter discusses how the U.S. market economy operates, focusing on both its promises and its problems. The next chapter talks about global economic issues.

A commitment to economic justice requires a clear-headed ability to evaluate the successes and failures of our own local and national economy. This can be difficult–we are *part* of this economy. Many of us have benefited greatly from the jobs, the income, and the wealth that the U.S. economy has generated. Many of us have also suffered from its recessions, unemployment, and unequally distributed opportunities.

A belief in the effectiveness of a "free market economy" is almost the equivalent of a religious faith among many Americans. As we shall see, the current U.S. economy is actually what is typically called a "mixed market economy." Although the market is the dominant form of economic organization, there are many areas in which we all accept and even expect that the market solutions will be overridden by government actions. In this, the United States is similar to all other Western countries. The difference between the United States economy and that of Japan, Britain, Sweden, or other Western countries, is in where and how the government regulates the market. All of these countries have mixed market economies.

It is clear that the United States is deeply committed to some form of market economy, thus this is the economic system that we discuss here. If we would seriously commit ourselves to seeking economic justice, we must be willing to name the injustices that occur around us, to criticize and reform our own economy. A confessional understanding of where we stand today may awaken a new sense of possibilities for change. Such confession is a statement of love: we care enough about the economy in which we live that we are willing to struggle with its transformation.

What Is a "Market Economy"?

Our economy is based on the concept of a competitive market. Adam Smith, a political philosopher who is known as the father of modern economics, first described this phenomenon in 1776 in his famous book, *The Wealth of Nations*. In its most condensed form, a market occurs when many buyers come together with many sellers and prices are set by a competitive bidding process. It is important to understand how a market economy works in order to understand also where the concept of "free markets" can fail. Let me provide a simple example of a competitive market.

Suppose that you and others are in the market for a new church hymnal, and therefore I decide to produce church hymnals for sale. Assume that I calculate that I must sell my hymnals for at least $12, in order to cover my production costs and pay myself an adequate salary. If you are interested in buying a hymnal, I might offer my hymnal to you at some price, say $20. Being an informed shopper, however, before you accept my offer you seek information on whether anyone else is offering the same hymnal at a lower price. Because other sellers will face pretty much the same production costs as I do, there is an incentive for another person to start producing hymnals and offer to sell them at $18. If this occurs, you and all other buyers will buy only from my competitor and not from me. Wanting to sell my hymnals, I lower my price to $16, which induces my competitor to lower the price to $14. Any of us can capture the market in hymnals if we sell at a lower price than anyone else. But none of us is willing to sell below $12, because then we start losing money. The result is that prices are bid down to $12, the lowest possible price at which hymnals can be effectively sold, which is called the *competitive price*. As long as you want a hymnal and are willing to pay at least $12 for it, a market in hymnals will exist.

We have each made a free choice to participate in this market. At $12, I meet my production costs and make an acceptable salary, therefore I am made better off by selling hymnals; your willingness to pay $12 for a hymnal implies that you want a hymnal badly enough that you would rather have the hymnal than the $12. That I choose to make and sell a hymnal and you choose to buy it implies that we have implicitly decided that we are both better off than we would be in a world where no hymnals were made or sold.

In reality, of course, buyers and sellers rarely gather together in an open marketplace, where such bidding occurs before everyone's eyes. However, because information flows freely and quickly, this process continues implicitly. If enough people want to buy a product, there is an economic incentive for someone to start producing and selling it. Thus, a market is created. Buyers seek the lowest available price for the product they want to buy; sellers who charge prices higher than their competitors are driven out of business or forced to lower prices. This occurs in the market for automobiles and groceries, as well as in the labor market where firms negotiate with workers over wages.

Adam Smith described this process as the "invisible hand." Everyone pursues his or her own self-interest. Sellers produce only goods that can be sold; buyers always seek the lowest price. No one directs what is bought or sold. Yet, as if an invisible hand were directing the process, buyers can find what they want and sellers can make a living producing it.

My favorite example of the invisible hand at work is my local Woolworth's store. I stop in at Woolworth's at least once a month to purchase small items for my office or home. Neither I nor any other customer ever telephones ahead of time to order things; nor does the owner of Woolworth's ever ask me what I expect to buy next month or what price I'm willing to pay. Yet I consistently find what I want somewhere on Woolworth's shelves, usually at a price that appears reasonable and affordable. (If a price seems high, I can always walk two blocks down the street to a different store and see if I can get the same item at a better price.) At Woolworth's, one can see the miracle of the market at work. Literally thousands of items are available for my purchase if I want them, without any conscious effort on my part. But my shopping patterns, combined with thousands of other Woolworth's customers, send the appropriate signals to producers as to how much to make and what price to charge.

This is an extremely simplified description of the basic workings of a pure market economy, but it should be enough to make the point that a market economy promises some significant benefits to its participants. In particular, there are at least four advantages that are often discussed:

1. Competitive prices. As my story about hymnals illustrates, as long as consumers are informed about comparative prices and as long as any producer can start into business, it will be difficult to overprice products and make excess profits. Someone who overcharges will be driven out of business when customers switch to a lower-priced competitor. The market process will bid prices down to their lowest sustainable level.

2. Free choice. There is no coercion in the hymnal market. You don't have to buy a hymnal and I don't have to produce one. We both enter the market only if it is in our interest to do so.

3. Incentives for efficient production. If I can produce a hymnal at a lower cost than my competitor, I can sell more hymnals. Therefore, there are always incentives for me to work more efficiently or to investigate new technologies that allow me to produce hymnals more cheaply. Productivity is encouraged.

4. No need for bureaucratic oversight. In the simple market story above, there is no need for a government of any sort. Everything occurs quite nicely through private transactions between buyers and sellers of hymnals. No extra money needs to be spent paying government regulators or bureaucrats to oversee the market.

Unfortunately, Things Aren't so Simple

Although the advantages of a properly functioning market economy can be very real, the "hymnal market" described above relies on certain assumptions about the world. There are a wide variety of situations in which the "invisible hand" does not work as neatly as our hymnal market example implies. In particular, the following six problems occur frequently in many market situations. When these problems arise, the advantages of the competitive market may no longer hold. In such cases, rather than leaving the market to function on its own, better economic decisions can be made when the community, operating through its government, explicitly intervenes in the market and overrides the invisible hand.

1. Lack of Information

One of the most frequent problems in market situations is lack of information on the part of potential customers. In the example above, the only reason I could not sell you a $20 hymnal is that you knew you could get an equivalent product from another seller for $18. If you had not known this, I could have exploited your lack of information and made my fortune selling you hymnals at $8 above the competitive price.

There are a wide variety of decisions in which consumers may not easily be able to acquire the information they need to make informed market decisions. Some products are complex, and a buyer learns about their quality only after they are purchased and used. For instance, you learn that your new car doesn't perform as well as promised only after you own it a while. Because it may be easy for a salesperson to explicitly provide misinformation about quality to a customer in this situation, there is a role for government to enforce regulations on the accuracy of information a customer is given. Thus, sales brochures cannot make false claims about their products. Speedometers on used cars can't be set back. Such regulations assure customers of accurate information and, therefore, produce better purchasing decisions than the private market could guarantee by itself.

There are many examples of situations in which we typically believe customers are better off when laws regulate the information the private market must provide. Milk cartons have "Sell before Jan 20" stamped on them for customers to see. Packaged foods have content labels. Over-the-counter drugs carry warning labels. Companies that expose their workers to risk of poisoning or injury without adequate warning or protection can be sued for damages. All of these are "interventions" in the market, designed to assure that sellers disclose full information about their products that they may not provide if left to pursue only their own self interest. The result of these laws and regulations is to improve the economic decisions of consumers.

2. Excess Economic Power

A crucial part of the market story is the assumption that there are many buyers and many sellers and no one has any more influence than anyone else. If I sell my hymnals at an unduly high price, I cannot stop competitors from producing hymnals and underselling me. Customers who don't like my product can always go to any other producer and are not forced to buy from me. In reality, of course, such an assumption is often untrue.

There are any number of situations in which sellers are able to gain excess market power. They may have the ability to either sell at a price well above the competitive price or to refuse to sell to certain customers. Grocery stores in inner-city neighborhoods often charge higher prices than those in wealthy neighborhoods. This is in part because these inner-city stores have a captive customer base. If inner-city residents lack easy transportation to other stores (toting groceries any distance on buses and subways can be extremely difficult), then the local store can charge higher prices because many customers have no other alternative. Some local governments have taken steps to actively encourage local grocery chains to locate stores in inner-city communities, thus increasing services and lowering prices for these residents.

At the extreme, some firms try aggressively to manipulate markets and exclude their competitors. Antitrust laws were established to control and prosecute such behavior, and such firms can be charged with "restraint of trade." When sellers pursue their own self-interests, it is necessarily to their advantage to get rid of their competitors. Inevitably, some persons will try to rig bids or fix deals. Many laws and regulations are designed to limit such behavior.

Sometimes, however, limits on competition are widely accepted. There are a variety of cases in which, as a society, working through our government, we limit consumer choice or establish "official monopolies." Zoning laws exclude certain types of businesses and residences from a particular area. Rules against private mail delivery enforce the monopoly of the post office. A single electric company operates in most communities. In these situations the government tries to control the effects of excess market power by regulating the prices charged by utility companies, cable companies, taxicabs, or the post office.

In short, when someone buys what another person sells, this may or may not be a situation of free choice, exercised at the lowest possible price. There are many situations in which the "choices" available to people are seriously constrained. In some cases this is judged "restraint of trade" and is illegal. In other cases, such as in a one-company town with but a single employer, we may try to offset the potential negative effects through law or government regulation. In still other cases, communities choose to support monopolies actively, believing that a single public utility serves a town better than multiple utility companies.

Simply calling for "free markets" everywhere in our economy ignores the real complexity of the world in which we live. Sometimes greater competition is a good thing. Sometimes we accept limited competition but try to offset its potential negative effects through laws or government regulation. When evaluating a particular market, it is always worth asking the following questions: How easy is it for competitors to enter this market? How easy is it for customers to buy from alternative producers? What advantages or disadvantages would occur if people's choices were constrained?

3. Externalities

If there is no excess market power, we typically assume that the price at which a customer buys and a seller sells is the competitive price. This price covers the producer's costs and reflects the buyer's need. There are, however, some transactions in which more people are affected than just the buyer and the seller. In this case, the private transaction between buyer and seller does not take account of the full social costs or benefits, and *externalities* can occur.

A positive externality occurs when other persons beyond the buyer and seller benefit from a transaction. When this happens, the price paid in the private market may be too high. An example occurs in the area of elementary and secondary education. If education were left to the private market, most people would purchase some of it for their children, but some people might not value it and some could not afford it. Leaving this decision to the private market, therefore, ignores the benefits to society of assuring that every child is literate. If I choose not to educate my children, my whole community is worse off—my children will be less productive and less informed citizens. For this reason, the government provides free (and mandatory) elementary and secondary schooling for all children. The positive benefits to society of basic schooling for all are too great to leave the decision to private market transactions.

A negative externality occurs when the private market ignores costs to others. The classic example is pollution. If a factory spews dirty smoke into the air, it imposes costs on everyone who lives nearby. If its products are sold 50 miles away where buyers are unaffected by the pollution, these costs can be ignored by the firm. In a sense, the price of the product is too low, because the pollution costs created by its production are ignored. Government regulations limiting the amount of smoke a plant can put in the air force the firm to "internalize" the external costs they have been imposing on their community. The firm will have to invest in pollution control equipment. This may result in higher prices, but these prices will now reflect the full cost of production.

In today's society, we accept government intervention in private markets because of externalities. Firms are forced to contribute to unemployment compensation funds, in order to internalize the social costs of unemployment that occur when they lay off workers. The government subsidizes the cost of school lunches for children, because society benefits when its future citizens have good nutrition and good health.

4. Public Goods

A number of government-provided services cannot be analyzed in a market framework at all. These are called public goods. They are typically bought and sold only by the government and, once they are available, can be used by all. They include everything from national defense, to parks, to police protection. It is impossible to determine how much of these goods to buy or what to pay for them using standard market tools.

A national defense system is an example. There is only one purchaser; only the government hires soldiers or buys MX missiles in the United States. And once the government has "bought" national defense, it cannot exclude any citizen from benefiting from this service. Coast Guard ships that patrol the territorial waters of the United States protect everyone. The national highway system is also a public good. Only the federal government "buys" interstate highways, and once highways are built, it is very difficult to exclude people from them. (Highways may be somewhat exclusionary, since one can charge tolls, regulating access through price.)

The decision on how much money to spend on public goods is entirely a social decision. There is no market that determines how many missiles we buy or at what price. Similarly, no market will tell us how many national parks we should "purchase" and preserve. These decisions are made through the political process and depend upon the political will for more missiles versus more parks. They also depend on our willingness to purchase any public goods at all. (We can always eliminate both the military and the parks and cut taxes, so we can all buy more for our families in the private market.) Economic analysis can perhaps provide information on the effects of buying more missiles or more parks. Ultimately, however, our national and social priorities, our government decision-making processes, and our willingness to fund public services are the factors that determine how much and what kind of public goods we buy.

5. Social Biases and Discrimination

In the standard market story, all that matters in the market is personal resources. If you have the money to buy my hymnal at the offered price, I sell it to you. If I have a hymnal for sale at the price you want to pay, you buy it from me. It does not matter who I am or who you are. Economic transactions are assumed to be color blind, sex blind, ethnic blind, and indifferent to all issues except that of quality and price.

Unfortunately, this model ignores social reality. The economy is located inside a nation's larger social and cultural habits, and economic decisions are as subject to social biases as any other type of decision. I recently held a job on the faculty at Princeton University. Had I applied to Princeton for a job twenty years ago with exactly the same training and abilities, I would never have been hired. Princeton would not have looked at my teaching and research skills twenty years ago because they had rule against hiring women.

All economic decisions are made in the context of the social patterns and behavior of the time. Most of our personal economic decisions are heavily conditioned by our cultural habits, from the clothes we buy to the food we eat. In a similar way, the decisions made by economic institutions—by schools, by businesses, by charitable organizations—are heavily influenced by cultural assumptions.

For instance, the assumption that "disabled persons cannot work" is based more on a stereotype about physical disability than on actual evidence. Yet because of this assumption, many persons with limits on physical mobility are denied jobs that require little physical exertion. Similarly, cultural assumptions about the productivity of older workers, African American youth, or married women with children affect employers' hiring. As a result, productive persons face limited work opportunities.

All too often, economic patterns that result from underlying social biases are ascribed to market forces. Persons who are observed in dead-end, limited-skill jobs are assumed to have somehow "chosen" these jobs. The myth that everything is governed by competitive markets leads to the conclusion that only the unproductive or lazy end up unemployed or in low-wage jobs. This ignores the social reality that economic decisions are influenced by discrimination and exclusion in the larger society.

6. No Attention to Adequacy

A market system is entirely blind to issues of individual well-being. Competitive markets describe how individuals earn income and buy products. There is, however, no guarantee in a market economy that the resulting income will be adequate for survival.

Many groups in society are outside the market. Most notably, children and elderly people–who make up half of all poor persons in the U.S. economy–are typically not expected to work. Without work, they have no income of their own. A just society establishes networks and systems that assure that the young and old are cared for. This in no way contradicts the workings of a competitive market. Market systems simply do not address the question of what happens to those outside the market. Family systems, community networks, and government income support programs are all part of a social consensus to care for the well-being of those who cannot work. The amount of money a society should spent on educational opportunities for children or on health care for the elderly cannot be determined by market forces. These are social decisions that depend on the community's sense of need and its political will to provide such services.

Even among those who seek work, the market system in

no way guarantees adequate income. If jobs are scarce, if one's English skills are poor, or if one's schooling was inadequate, full-time work may not earn enough to support a family. In 1991 a person who worked full-time year-round at the minimum wage of $4.25 earned only $8500. We frequently and actively intervene in the labor market because we care about issues of minimal adequacy. We provide job training programs, supplement income for the unemployed, create public sector jobs, provide tax subsidies to low-wage workers, or enforce a minimum wage. All of these policies override the outcome of the private labor market, which would leave many unemployed or low-skilled workers without the resources to support themselves or their families.

The Government and the Market

As the preceding discussion indicates, the United States is indeed a mixed market economy. Government interventions in the economy are common and widely acceptable. Virtually no one supports abolishing pollution controls or eliminating unemployment subsidies. The argument is instead over two questions: When should government rules override market outcomes? What type of government intervention should occur?

The discussion in chapter 3 indicated that there are many examples of economic exclusion, economic pain, and economic injustice in this country's economy. In some cases, these occur because of the failure of the market to correct one or more of the problems cited earlier in this chapter. In other cases, despite efforts to improve on market solutions, we lack either the knowledge or the political will to implement fully effective social programs.

Government intervention, per se, is hardly a guaranteed solution for economic injustice. There are some highly successful government programs that strengthen the economy and improve the lives of our citizens. But just as markets often perform ineffectively if left to themselves, so government programs can also be ineffective in reaching the goals they seek to achieve. As we have seen, however, leaving markets unregulated is often not a desirable alternative.

The challenge is to pursue effective government policies that improve economic outcomes.

There are a wide variety of ways in which a community, through its common political decisions, can choose to regulate the economy:

1. *Complete government ownership* of certain industries is used more frequently in European economies, but even in the United States the federal government directly owns and runs the post office and the National Park Service, and state and local governments own and run public schools and universities.

2. *Direct government regulation* occurs when regulations are established that monitor and enforce certain types of behavior in the private market. Product labeling requirements, antidiscrimination laws, child labor laws, and pollution control are all forms of mandatory government regulation.

3. *Incentive systems* are a more indirect form of government regulation. Incentive systems designed to improve individual or social behavior include fines for littering, rewards for persons who report crimes, tax rebates for persons who install energy-conserving heating systems, and special tax benefits for firms that locate in depressed economic areas.

4. In some cases, *public encouragement* for certain behavior is given, without rewards or mandates. Examples are warning labels on cigarettes, public announcements against drinking and driving, and informal "jawboning" by major public figures urging firms to maintain low prices or avoid large-scale layoffs.

5. *Government programs to provide economic support* for persons in need also crucially affect the economy. For instance, the government provides income and medical care to elderly and disabled persons through Social Security and the Medicare system. Food stamps provide food assistance to low-income households, and unemployment benefits are available to many unemployed workers.

There is a wide range of opinion about which forms of government intervention are best for the economy. Some support far more widespread government regulation and ownership as a way to increase social control over economic decision making. Others argue that there are serious problems in running large government programs and that incentive and encouragement programs, aimed at changing behavior voluntarily, are more effective.

Funding Government Activity

Government activity is funded by taxes. Just as there is no way to determine, through the market, the appropriate level of government spending on the military or on parks, so there is also no way of determining what the tax rate "ought to" be. If we as a society want increased government services, then we must be willing to accept higher taxes. Of course, money paid in taxes for government services can result in reduced private expenditures. For instance, a nationally run system of health care in this country would probably require substantially increased government revenues, but would reduce the private expenditures of businesses and individuals who fund their own health insurance.

Despite complaints about high taxes in this country, the United States has one of the lowest tax rates of any industrialized nation. Among the twenty-four wealthiest economies in the world, the United States collects a smaller share of taxes out of total national income than any other country except Japan. The United States also has less extensive public assistance programs than many of these other countries—and a higher poverty rate. There is nothing inherently bad about higher taxes or inherently good about lower taxes. If higher taxes purchase effective services that taxpayers want, then their economic effects will be positive. If they go to support corrupt or ineffective government actions, then they will have negative effects on the economy.

Assuring Effective Government Action

Any proposal to increase government involvement in the economy must be concerned about the effectiveness of these programs. Economic justice is not improved when government programs are wasteful and inefficient. In fact, the political will necessary to support efforts to improve the lives of needy citizens can be greatly lessened when people see money spent on ineffective programs.

A community that chooses to emphasize equity issues and implement government programs to redistribute income and enforce social standards on such issues as pollution, unsafe workplaces, unannounced plant closures, and so forth, must take seriously the following problems:

1. Unequal access to government decision making. Government decisions may be just as open to corruption and discriminatory behavior as private market decisions. Political structures are just as imbedded in the social fabric of a nation as economic structures, and just as subject to the same cultural biases. The primary difference, in a democratic government, is that all persons interested in an issue are promised a voice in government decision making, access that is often not available in private market decisions. If access to government decisions is limited or government decisions are exclusionary or corrupt, movement toward greater government involvement in the economy may increase injustice.

2. Lack of information by government bureaucracies. Governments are not all-knowing. The same informational problems that can cause bad economic decisions in private markets can also lead the government to make bad decisions. Some information is simply never available. But the government has the ability in some cases to enforce the centralized collection of information much more readily than private participants in a market.

3. Incentive problems. Because government decisions are not made in the context of a market, there is often less incentive for productivity or efficiency in government-run programs than in private markets. Thus, the concern over waste in government programs can be justified. The economies of eastern Europe, which for many years pursued an economic system of complete government ownership of virtually all firms, have demonstrated some of the inadequacies of leaving all economic decisions to large government bureaucracies. Government bureaucracies can become enmeshed in pursuing the particular goals of those who run them, rather than the well-being of their clients and customers. (Of course, this is not a unique problem to government, as the recent savings and loan scandal indicates.) Still, inefficiency need not be inherent in government programs. There are many effective and well-run government programs. Widespread citizen monitoring and participation in government decision making and institutions can serve as a check on government behavior. Clear performance goals are also often useful, along with opportunities for feedback and outside review.

Balancing the Demands of Justice

A commitment to economic justice provides no easy answers as to how such justice is to be achieved in a complex modern economy. Unregulated competitive markets often produce economic outcomes that few in society would find acceptable. The government can play an important role in addressing some of these private market inadequacies, but government programs also require citizen involvement and effective leadership in order to be effective.

There is no perfect economic system, awaiting a timely implementation. The United States has adopted a mix of competitive markets and government intervention, recognizing that each has problems, but each can also complement the other. Some western European countries have made a similar choice to mix market and government-controlled economic systems, although many of these countries have opted for a mix that provides greater government involvement than in the United States economy.

A commitment to economic justice necessarily implies a commitment to the redistribution of economic resources so that the poor and the dispossessed are more fully included in the economic system. I personally believe that this will require a greater shift away from market solutions and toward greater government involvement in economic decision making. As many of the western European economies indicate, the government can be far more involved in assuring jobs and income to low-income families than they are presently in the United States. The challenge for those of us who support such changes is to see that government expansion leads to improvements rather than to simply a different set of problems.

Most American Christians are deeply involved in the economic system of this country. For better or worse, few have either the knowledge or inclination to change drastically the entire structure of economic relations. For many middle-income Americans, the U.S. economy has produced at least a comfortable, if not a rich, life. This comfort often makes it difficult to be objective about the problems of that economy.

We are, however, children of a God who reveals a deep concern about economic injustice and economic exclusion. Because we are called to share this concern, we are called to engage in active and ongoing evaluation of the economy of which we are a part and to speak of its inequities and injustices when we see them. We are called to be informed and active citizens, using the opportunities available to work toward reform and improvement in this economy.

Working on reform and change within the current economic system is an important job. It should be clearly noted, however, that for a substantial minority such a call will seem inadequate. Those who have been most hurt and excluded by the system are far harsher in their criticisms and far more expansive in their calls for change.

Some persons will feel called to envision and support more radical change, seeking alternate and new economic systems. The church has always been a place where prophets speak, despite the discomfort such speech inevitably causes. The church must provide a forum for those who are led to work for economic transformation rather than economic reform. And all those concerned with economic issues must listen openly to such indictments of the present system and seriously consider the need for fundamental economic change.

Summary

This chapter looks critically at how the United States market economy is structured. An economic system that assures justice and prosperity for all has yet to be devised. In the United States, we have a mixed market system, in which we rely on competitive markets to determine prices and allocate goods. We choose to constrain the behavior of these markets in many ways to assure better economic decisions in cases in which the private market allocation is inadequate. The issue is not whether the government should be involved in economic decisions, but how to assure that the government does this in an effective way. Although a wide range of potential government interventions are possible, these programs are also subject to corruption, lack of information, and incentive problems. Economic reform in the United States that calls for greater involvement of government in the redistribution of resources and the well-being of American citizens must also be concerned about good management and effective implementation of government programs. Those who would go beyond reform envision more radical transformation and change.

GROUP DISCUSSION AND ACTIVITIES

Suggested Group Exercise

Photocopy the questionnaire on page 72 to provide one copy per participant. Have each person individually read the instructions and fill in the columns. Then, as a group, discuss each topic and reasons individuals had for choosing a particular answer.

Starting Discussion Questions

1. Go through the six types of market failure listed in this chapter. Provide specific examples in which you observe

this problem in a daily economic situation. Provide examples of government programs designed to solve such problems.

2. Discuss the pros and cons of the five different types of government intervention. Which would you use and when?

3. Discuss the problems of effectively implementing government programs (the chapter presents three specific problems.) Describe particular examples of effective or ineffective government programs with which you are familiar. How can these problems be avoided?

4. The author of this chapter states that she believes the government should be more involved in economic decision making, particularly in the redistribution of resources to the needy. Do you agree or disagree? Why?

5. It has been said that the problem of poverty, in a nation as rich as the United States, has little to do with economics and is entirely a matter of public and political will. Do you agree? How is political will created or mobilized?

Questionnaire on Government Intervention

Check the column that best represents your belief as to the right amount of public intervention, and indicate which level of government, if any, should have jurisdiction.

Column 1: No government regulation or intervention. Any oversight should be left to private industry and citizen groups.

Column 2: Government should impose some laws or regulations.

Column 3: Complete government control and operation.

	1	2	3
Air pollution	___	___	___
Stock market	___	___	___
Building construction	___	___	___
Newspapers, other media	___	___	___
Religious attendance	___	___	___
Law enforcement	___	___	___
Medical care	___	___	___
Car production	___	___	___
Shopping mall location	___	___	___
Elementary schools	___	___	___

CHAPTER 6
The United States and the Global Economy

A child born in India in 1985 had a 50 percent chance of being part of a family with an income of less than $1 per day, and a 20 percent chance of dying before age 5. Such extreme poverty occurs throughout the poorest nations. At the other end of the spectrum, many citizens of the industrialized nations have annual incomes that are counted in the tens of thousands of dollars. In between lie a large number of middle-income countries, such as Mexico, Egypt, and Malaysia, that do not have the wealth of the United States, but most of whose citizens are not desperately poor. What determines a country's level of income and wealth? Why have some countries remained poor, while in other countries the health, income, and skills of the population have increased steadily? This chapter discusses the global economy, with particular attention to the causes of economic development and income growth and to the role of the United States in the global economy.

An American Dilemma

It is difficult for Americans to grapple with the issue of world income differentials. The economic gap between middle-income American life and the utter poverty of sub-Saharan Africa is so vast that it is morally impossible to justify. For most of us, it was an accident of birth that made us citizens of one of the richest and most powerful nations in history. How do we understand a world in which invisible national boundaries are the primary determinant of whether a child shall die young or live a long and healthy life? Because it is so difficult for faithful Americans to think about these issues without feeling confused, unworthy, or overwhelmingly guilty, the temptation is to ignore them.

Unfortunately, this chapter has no conclusive answers to the ethical question of how a middle-income American lives a faithful and a moral life in a world with such differentials in wealth. At best, this chapter can suggest some directions for action and thought that may be useful. We start with a recognition that our economic and political choices as Americans fundamentally affect the lives of people around the globe.

Connections Around the Globe

The United States emerged as a major world political and economic leader in the twentieth century. Today, multinational corporations headquartered in the United States oversee vast amounts of business around the world. The United States imports more goods from abroad than any other country. The U.S. government is also a leading player in negotiations over political and economic issues throughout the globe. Most recently, the United States has been a source of advice and assistance for the newly independent eastern European countries as they struggle to find a new political and economic shape for themselves. The U.S. economy is a critical part of the world economy; other nations' economies are affected by the strength of the U.S. dollar, the rate of U.S. inflation, and the amount of U.S. development assistance.

Because of the role that the United States plays in the global economy, our lives as American citizens are bound up with the lives of the rich and poor around the globe. On the one hand, we are involved as citizens in shaping and approving the foreign and economic policy of the U.S. government. On the other hand, we are also involved in the world economy through our private economic choices. We buy products made around the world: Colombian coffee, Japanese TVs, T-shirts from Taiwan, and jewelry from Nigeria. In addition, many of us regularly do business with or directly work for a wide variety of companies that operate throughout the world.

Recent Economic Changes Around the Globe

At a global level, there has clearly been good news over the past three decades. Since the early 1960s, both high-income and low-income countries have, on average, experienced increases in income and literacy, and declines in infant mortality and population growth rates. Although the level of global poverty remains shockingly high, the world has become somewhat less poor over the past few decades. Beneath these average figures, however, there is enormous change and diversity. The United States and western Europe have been joined by Japan as the wealthiest industrialized nations, many of whose citizens have comfortable middle-class incomes. Other countries, such as Korea, Israel, and Saudi Arabia, have also experienced dramatic income growth and improved living standards. Some countries, such as Brazil and the eastern European nations, have shown much more uncertain progress in recent decades, following earlier and faster income growth. Many poor countries have become somewhat less poor, such as China, Pakistan, and Indonesia, and a few very poor countries have become poorer, such as Chad and Uganda. Why are some nations able to improve their economic situation, while others remain mired in poverty? The answer to this question is crucial, since it may indicate ways to lessen world poverty in the years ahead.

The economist's way of phrasing this question is to ask,"What causes economic growth and development?" Social scientists have debated this issue for years, looking at what differentiates the wealthier and more industrially developed countries from the poorer developing world. A variety of explanations have been offered, which we will briefly explore.

Theory 1: Resource Differences

The theory of resource differences claims that some nations become wealthy simply because they are fortunate enough to possess natural resources that others want to buy or that are useful in supporting a growing economy. South Africa is richer than Zimbabwe because it has deposits of gold and diamonds. Iran is wealthier than Turkey because of its oil deposits. The United States is wealthier than Mexico because of its rich agricultural land and its many deposits of coal, oil, and other natural resources.

Although there is clearly some truth in this theory, by itself it is inadequate to explain the great differences in wealth between countries. Many small nations with few natural resources, such as Japan and England, have acquired enormous economic and political wealth. In addition, even lands richly blessed in natural resources, such as Cambodia, have experienced serious poverty. Increasingly, natural resources seem less important than human resources in the world economy; education and human skill can more than compensate for a lack of oil or coal. Although rich endowments of natural resources almost surely have given certain countries a head start in economic development and growth, this offers only a partial and inadequate explanation of world patterns of development.

Theory 2: Market Development Theory

The traditional economic explanation for development is that market economies create wealth when they are allowed to function freely. As the feudal European economies became "marketized"—transformed from subsistence agriculture to modern industrial economies—wealth was accumulated through the process of savings and investment. A market economy creates incentives for producers to improve and expand their business. It creates incentives for persons to become literate and acquire skills. Some have claimed that this inevitably leads to increased industrialization, which means growing markets, expanding trade, and rising national wealth. Thus, the way to economic growth is by opening up markets, seeking capital investment to stimulate new jobs and new businesses, and allowing the entrepreneurial spirit of the population to emerge and generate jobs and wealth.

Although this story is consistent with some of the historical facts of European and American development, its application to many other nations' more recent efforts at development is unclear. American and European industrial development occurred gradually over more than a century. In the post-World War II era, countries go through this process (or fail to go through it) in only a few decades. Some nations that were predicted to become fully industrialized and wealthy economies—such as Brazil—have failed to live up to expectations. Other nations, such as the small island nations of Singapore or Taiwan, have exceeded expectations.

It has become clear that industrial development is a very complex process, and there is nothing that guarantees it will proceed along a particular track once it begins. Some nations have industrialized certain segments of their economy, but rather than spreading and creating more income and wealth for everyone, their economies instead have segmented and stagnated, creating great divisions in income and well-being among different groups. Initiating movement toward a market economy does not guarantee that long-term growth will flourish.

On the one hand, the traditional tools of economic development clearly matter: a nation's wealth tends to increase faster the more money available for capital investment, the greater the market for a country's products, or the more educated the labor force. On the other hand, this process is more difficult to start and harder to continue than traditional market economic theory often suggests.

Theory 3: Dependency Theory

Dependency theory claims that the differences in wealth and development between countries are due to the historical patterns of political and economic power between nations. In particular, some nations become wealthy because they are powerful enough to exploit poorer nations. Poor nations stay poor because wealthier and more powerful nations benefit by limiting their economic wealth and power. Thus, in this view of the world, Europe is rich *because* Africa is poor, and Latin America is poor *because* the United States is rich.

The historical basis of these exploitative economic processes was the colonial system, in which European countries used the cheap labor and natural resources of their colonies to increase their own wealth, without returning any of this wealth to the colonial nations from which they took it. A necessary part of this enforced economic powerlessness among the colonies was also enforced political powerlessness. The colonial powers established governments that often treated native citizens as inferior in their own land.

Although most former colonies have been independent for many years, proponents of dependency theory argue that the colonial arrangements have continued indirectly. First, multinational corporations (headquartered in and potentially run for the benefit of the former colonial powers) continue to exercise powerful control over the economies of poorer nations. Second, the former colonial powers continue to maintain political control over their "power block" by assuring that political leaders are selected in these countries who can be controlled and influenced. Thus, it is claimed that a wide variety of rather unsavory political leaders have been supported because they furthered the political and economic interests of the developed world.

Colonialism was undoubtedly exploitative, but it is far from clear that dependency theory explains economic development in the postcolonial world. It does not explain how some excolonies have been able to emerge as economically strong and independent nations. It does not explain the lack of development in many countries of Africa that threw off their colonial status at least thirty years ago and that are not part of any larger nation's clear "power block." There is also little empirical evidence over the past few decades that economic growth in the industrialized world was in any way dependent upon poverty and dependency in the developing world. In fact, those countries that have experienced significant development are clearly more important to the economic well-being of the industrialized world than the poorest countries.

Still, this conflicting evidence notwithstanding, there are elements of dependency theory that can be compelling. The economic health of some number of countries–particularly those that export only a single major raw material–remains precariously dependent on the political and economic decisions of larger and wealthier countries. And the industrialized world continues to exercise its military, political, and economic power at will throughout the world, often in ways that pay scant attention to the needs of the poor populations that are affected.

Theory 4: Domestic Political Structure

Another theory claims that the primary determinant of economic growth is a country's internal political structure and the interests it pursues. In countries where political control is maintained by an "elite class," government and economic decisions are often designed to promote the well-being of only the wealthiest citizens, which may stifle economic growth in the long run. For instance, the owners of the large plantations in Central America typically reinvested their wealth in luxury goods for themselves, rather than reinvesting in productive capital. The local governments, run by similar groups of elites, supported this behavior. In contrast, economic development in the United States was clearly linked to the broad-based land ownership and political participation in this country in earlier time periods. The government had to be responsive to the interests of the very broad group of small farmers and merchants who composed American society in the last century and who were active in its politics.

It has been noted that almost all nations in the currently industrialized world have at least semidemocratic systems, with broad voting rights. In contrast, nations ruled by dictators, or by small groups who value the interests of only a narrow portion of society, appear to experience far more problems with development. For instance, dictatorial governments with little concern for the broad common good are often cited as primary examples of why certain African nations have not been successful since decolonization. It seems that governments controlled by narrow interests are unable to develop thriving economies.

This theory also has its limits. Several of the thriving small Asian countries, which have recently experienced very rapid development, have done so under quite restrictive and semidictatorial governments. It is also clear that in the history of the United States and certain European nations, the government was frequently responsive to only very narrow groups in society. It seems, however, that the internal political conditions of a country are at least one important component of its economic progress.

Theory 5: Social/Cultural Background

A final theory about development focuses on the social and cultural background of a country as the determining cause of its economic growth. Many have argued that certain cultures are better suited than others for industrialization or economic development. Perhaps the most famous book on this topic, written by Max Weber in the early part of this century, argued that the American Protestant ethic (including a belief that hard work is always rewarded) made it possible for capitalism and industrialization to flourish in this country. Similarly, some have argued that the cultural background of certain Asian societies, emphasizing the values of discipline, education, and hard work, has been the main reason that some of the Asian nations have been so successful in increasing their wealth. In contrast, some argue that the Spanish culture brought to South America during colonization has slowed down and limited economic growth in that region.

These are difficult arguments to document, because "culture" is such a complex and unmeasurable concept. In addition, some are disturbed because an argument that claims "certain cultures are economically more successful," can often shade over into an argument that claims "if this group just worked harder they would be more economically successful," ignoring other structural and institutional constraints. However, it is surely true that economic behavior cannot be separated from its social and cultural context. The racism imbedded in American culture has created economic barriers for African Americans, just as ethnic and religious rivalries in other societies have excluded various groups from jobs and leadership.

The debate about the underlying causes of economic growth and development will clearly continue for many years. In fact, a single "true" explanation is probably illusory. All of the theories described above may be more or less correct in different countries at different points in history. Economic development is a complex process that can be aided and hindered by many factors.

Is "Development" a Good Thing?

Some readers will be unhappy with the discussion so far: I have talked about industrialization and economic growth as the preferred outcome for poor nations. This assumption is itself controversial. There are those who argue that Western styles of development are not good models for the future. Western industrialization has wasted resources, threatened the environment, and paid too little attention to the well-being of workers. Market economies may widen the gap between the rich and the poor, as some groups accumulate wealth faster.

On the other hand, there is a danger in romanticizing economies whose members are caught in abject poverty. Subsistence agriculture requires strenuous and often health-breaking labor, offering uncertain and meager rewards. Industrialized countries have found a way to provide the majority of their citizens with enough income to assure decent housing, food, education, and transportation, although there are still millions who are excluded from these benefits.

One of the real challenges for those who work on economic growth in poor countries is to seek routes to development that deal more humanely with workers, that are not destructive of traditional cultures, and that avoid environmental destruction. Unfortunately, any form of social change—and industrialization and market growth often involve vast social change—is typically painful, threatening people with situations they are unprepared to face. At some level, such pain is unavoidable if an economy is to undergo change.

Defining Economic Development More Broadly

It is important to recognize that "economic development" should include far more than just growth in a nation's aggregate income. There are at least three additional aspects of economic development that are crucial, beyond the continuing accumulation of income and wealth in a country:

1. The overall *distribution* of growth and well-being. If growing incomes are received by only a limited group in the population, this may create greater economic injustice.

2. Measures of *family well-being beyond income.* Declines in infant mortality rates, illiteracy, disease, homelessness, and malnutrition are just as important as increases in cash income. For instance, China produced an enormous improvement in the well-being of its population in the 1970s, not by raising family incomes, but by providing health and education services to all rural villages.

3. Long-term responsible use of *environmental resources.* Countries that increase their short-term wealth by destroying or using up natural resources may limit their ability to sustain such growth.

Only when economic growth is understood to necessarily include these aspects, as well as growth in total national wealth, is economic development a clearly desirable goal.

What Role Should the Developed Nations Play?

Given the complexity of the development process, what is the appropriate role for more developed nations, such as the United States, in encouraging development among poorer countries? There are at least three lessons in this discussion of economic development.

First, many aspects of development depend on internal national decisions and can be only indirectly affected by other nations. No "outsider" nation can or should be entirely responsible for intervening in the political structure, cultural attributes, or public choices made by other nations, particularly if those choices reflect decisions involving broad participation.

Second, external influences on national economies are, nonetheless, extensive and important. Outside capital and investment support may make it possible for fledgling industries to survive. Outside aid to assist a country that is trying to provide more widespread educational opportunities or health improvements may be necessary. International support for a government trying to decrease ethnic strife, discrimination, or human rights abuses can be crucial.

Knowing when to give assistance and in what ways, and knowing when to avoid intervening or influencing the national course of events is a difficult, if not impossible, art. Both nations, such as the United States, as well as international organizations, such as the United Nations, need to find better ways to exercise discretion and judgment in their assistance to developing countries.

Third, a concern with the broader aspects of development beyond income growth implies that nations and organizations providing development aid must be concerned with the needs of the poor and the distribution of resources in recipient countries. Too often, development aid has focused on projects designed to make average income grow, without giving attention to who would benefit and who would lose. In many cases, the United States has been too eager to support the agenda of existing political power groups in developing countries, without attention to the poor. The international community can also speak for those who may not have political voice in a country. For instance, in the late 1970s the United States initiated a requirement that the State Department write a human rights report for every nation that receives aid and make the results of that report a part of ongoing aid negotiations with a country. Such a policy explicitly supports those who are facing abuse and prods national governments to pay attention to human rights issues.

Key Global Economic Issues for the United States

Because of the political leadership and dominant economic position of the United States in the world, its actions are important. This is both because of the potential direct impact of U.S. decisions on poorer nations and because of the role of the United States as a model and world leader for other countries. The United States is also a primary participant in international organizations such as the World Bank or the United Nations, whose actions and regulations substantially affect the developing world. There are a number of areas in which the United States plays a key role in decisions that heavily affect the developing world.

Trade Policy. The United States is the largest importer of products from developing countries. It is also a key negotiator in international tariff negotiations. (Tariffs are taxes on goods imported from another country.) Many developing countries have difficulty in finding markets for their products because of trade barriers imposed by more developed nations. Importing nations often set explicit import quotas or tariffs. In particular, many countries use "escalated tariffs," tariffs that are higher for goods involving greater processing. This makes it difficult for developing countries to shift away from the export of raw materials and start developing their own manufacturing and processing industries internally. The World Bank estimates that trade liberalization would substantially benefit middle-income developing countries. For the poorest countries, the advantages of trade liberalization depend heavily on their ability to adjust to a different world trade environment, which depends on debt relief.

Debt Relief. Many of the poorest countries borrowed heavily from international banks and from richer countries in the 1970s, largely in response to a severe world-wide recession following the sharp rise in oil prices. As a result, the debt burden–the amount of money paid out annually to cover interest on debt–is enormous for some of these countries. In several African countries, annual interest payments total more than 50 percent of their outside development aid, which means that the industrialized countries receive much of their aid back directly in debt payments, severely limiting any effect of such aid on reducing poverty and stimulating economic growth. In recent years a number of international initiatives have been aimed at helping poor countries reduce their debt burden, including debt forgiveness and debt rescheduling. The United States has played a major role in determining the scope and nature of these efforts.

Development Aid. The United States, like other wealthy nations, provides substantial amounts of foreign aid to poor countries. The United States gives more dollars of development aid than almost any other country, but because the U.S. economy is so large, this constitutes a relatively small share of its budget. The United Nations has called upon its wealthier member nations to each give 1 percent of their GNP to poorer countries in the form of development aid. (This is the international equivalent of tithing.) Among the eighteen most industrialized countries that belong to the Organization of Economic Cooperation and Development, the United States ranks seventeenth, giving only one-fifth of 1 percent of its GNP in development aid, behind Japan, the United Kingdom, France, Germany, and others. This percentage has been steadily declining over the last two decades.

Development aid can be crucial to poor countries as a source of external funding for economic development efforts. However, evaluations of the effectiveness of development aid in helping reduce poverty in recipient countries are quite mixed. In some cases this is the fault of the recipient country, when it uses the funds on projects that contribute to the well-being of only a narrow group of citizens. In other cases, the fault lies with the donor countries who insist on certain types of projects and who do not hold recipient governments accountable for assuring that such aid is used for programs targeted for the poor. Just providing aid dollars may not be enough. The U.S. government needs to take responsibility for seeing that these dollars are used effectively and in ways that diminish poverty and improve the lives of the poor in the recipient countries.

Transnational Corporations

The actions of the United States government are not the only connection that U.S. citizens have with the international economy. Many of us also work for and buy from a wide variety of companies that operate worldwide. These transnational corporations are major participants in the global economy. In some cases they are larger than some of the small countries with whom they do business. If General Motors were a country, considering sales equivalent to gross national income, it would be the twentieth richest country in the world.

Transnational corporations provide international markets for goods. In many cases they provide export opportunities for poor countries, which generates needed income for these countries. Transnational corporations, however, are necessarily focused on their own profitability and are less concerned with the social and developmental goals of poorer countries. This sometimes means that their behavior can impede long-term development. It also means that their interests are sometimes best promoted through dictatorial governments who promise long-term stable market contracts. Further, it means that their strategies may exclude or impoverish groups who lack the interest or ability to be part of their markets.

It would require a book in itself to discuss the entire range of questions relating to the behavior and regulation of transnational companies. In general, there are two points to be made. First, there is a need to monitor the behavior and regulate the activities of private corporations. Different countries have different needs, but through tax and legislative policy, governments of developing countries have encouraged foreign-owned companies to promote local workers into management positions, decreased tax avoidance, negotiated long-term contracts to guarantee steady export income, and improved workers' wages and working conditions. Yet, it may be possible for smaller and poorer nations to impose regulations on large international companies. This means there is a role for international regulations, negotiated by an organization such as the United Nations, with participation by the private companies, the poorer nations, and the nations where these companies are headquartered.

Second, there is a need for private corporations to see themselves as ethical entities, as well as profit-making businesses. Companies are involved in the communities and the lives of their workers. Therefore, they have responsibilities to those workers and communities. For example, in the past decade many internationally owned companies that operate in South Africa have changed their practices in order to promote and train more black workers or to assure their workers' families adequate education and housing.

Most managers of large corporations are good and well-intentioned persons who try to behave fairly to others. It is important, however, to realize that corporate ethics involve more than just ethical behavior on the part of individual corporate managers. Well-intentioned and responsible individual actions do not guarantee ethical corporate behavior. A corporation is itself an entity, and its actions affect the lives of many persons. Corporate leaders need to consider the ethical and moral implications of decisions more broadly than is usual in a hierarchical decision-making process.

Think Globally

Perhaps the most important lesson of this chapter can be summarized in two words: Think globally. Our economic and political choices in America are linked to the economic well-being and choices of other people around the globe. Sometimes it's easy to see these connections, sometimes it's not.

When making policy choices at the global level, as well as at the national level, it is legitimate to ask, "What will this do for the poor?" U.S. foreign policy is affected by many things: political alliances, historical commitments, U.S. economic interests, and so on. In addition, it can be influenced by a group of citizens who regularly demand that it also ask the question "What does this do for (or against) the poorer nations of the world?"

In our own lives, thinking globally means including concerns about faraway neighbors in regular prayer and worship. It means being aware of the relationship between our individual economic choices and the well-being of others. It means considering the perspective of persons from other countries and other cultures. It may mean changes in what we buy and from whom we buy. It means a greater awareness of the world around us.

Think globally!

Summary

The economic disparities around the globe are enormous. Although the magnitude of global poverty and need can seem overwhelming, Americans in particular cannot retreat from this issue. As citizens of a powerful world economic leader, we are deeply tied to the economies of nations around the globe. Economic development in poor countries is a difficult and uncertain task. There are many theories as to why some countries become wealthier, while others remain poor. Whatever the underlying causes, however, it is clear that the international community can assist poor countries. Yet it is important to realize that economic development means more than income growth, that it also includes attention to the distribution of resources, family well-being, and the environment.

American citizens are linked to the international economy through the U.S. government and its involvement with other countries in trade, debt relief, and development aid. Americans are also involved because we are all consumers of international products. Many of us also work for and buy from large transnational corporations, that operate throughout the world and have a major influence on the economic well-being of many poorer and smaller nations. There is a need to develop new and better models of appropriate corporate behavior and regulation at an international level.

GROUP DISCUSSION AND ACTIVITIES

Suggested Group Exercise

Collect a number of headline stories about national or international events from local newspapers over the past week. Divide participants into small groups. Tell members of each group that they are citizens of a small and very poor country. Give each group a news story, and ask them to read it and discuss how members interpret it from the perspective of their country. What might this story tell them about the United States? What implications might it have for their own country? Would they write this story any differently for their own newspaper than it has been written for a U.S. newspaper? After ten minutes, call everyone together and, in the original large group, discuss how the perspectives of the small countries differed from the perspectives of Americans reading these same news stories.

Starting Discussion Questions

1. Consider the five theories of development presented in this chapter. For each theory, think of some examples that seem to support it. You may use examples from American history or draw on the histories of any other countries with which your are familiar.

2. From your knowledge of American history or the history of any other country you know, discuss the costs of development. Think of examples in which industrialization and economic growth left some individuals worse off. This chapter suggests that "development" should mean more than income growth. Do you agree with the three additional aspects of development that the author proposes?

3. Some persons argue that all development aid should be given with no strings attached; that is, countries can spend it any way they like once they receive it. Others argue that the donor country has a responsibility to see that recipient countries spend their aid effectively. These persons argue that aid should be tied to specific projects or that its use should meet certain criteria. Discuss the pros and cons of the United States directly regulating the ways in which its development aid to poorer nations might be spent.

4. What might it mean if "corporate ethics" involved more than the ethical behavior of individual workers in the corporation? Do you agree or disagree with this suggestion by the author?

CHAPTER 7

Christian Life in a World of Economic Choices

This book has argued that our economic lives cannot be separated from our religious lives. The next three chapters are designed to come to grips with the following two questions: If we are to link our economic and religious lives, what changes will this imply for our religious life? If we are to link our economic and religious lives, what changes will this imply for our economic life? This chapter focuses on economic and spiritual issues relating to personal lifestyle, and the next two chapters focus on the church community and our public and political communities.

Implications of the Link Between Faith and Economics

If all of our life is subject to God's care, God's support and concern, and God's judgment, this includes the range of economic problems and decisions that confront us. There are several implications. First, this framework places economic concerns in their proper perspective. Neither our income, our possessions, nor our job are of primary importance. Our primary concern is to live a life in accord with the wholeness and holiness toward which God calls each of us. When our economic life is in harmony with our Christian faith, we are no longer dominated by greed or pride in possessions. We are freed to reorder our priorities and activities. We are not controlled by the things we possess nor the things we want to possess.

This message is particularly important for Americans who are surrounded with many material comforts. We must be clear who and what we worship. When the pursuit of material well-being and personal possessions becomes our primary concern, we have replaced our Christian commitments with golden idols.

Second, recognizing that economic actions are also faith actions puts constraints on our behavior. We are not free to view our economic choices as purely private and justifiably self-interested decisions. We are all part of a larger household. Our economic decisions do not affect just ourselves and our family, but they also affect others. In this sense, our economic lifestyle–our charitable giving, our time commitments, our shopping habits, our work behavior–involves religious and spiritual choices as well as economic choices.

What Do We Choose?

We are all, by necessity, involved in economics. We make economic decisions for ourselves and our family on a daily basis. As Americans, many of us have the luxury of being able to make real *choices* about what we will buy, what job we will seek, or where we will live.

Yet all of us, and especially those with lower incomes, often feel buffeted and controlled by larger economic forces; our economic decisions often seem dictated by the necessities of our lives and not open to conscious choice. We *have to* find employment; we *have to* pay the rent; we *have to* own a car so we can get to work so we can earn money so we can pay the rent. How can we make changes in our economic lives if we have no choice or control?

First, it is worth remembering at this point that "economic life" includes a broad range of issues: It includes such things as which bills we pay and what job we work on. It also includes what we buy at the grocery store, at which grocery store we shop, what we give to the church, and how much time we spend in volunteer activities. In this sense, virtually all Americans have a range of economic choices in their lives.

Second, many of the things that feel like "oughts" and "have tos" in our life today are the results of choices we made yesterday. The couple who choose to buy a new car today typically commit themselves to monthly loan repayments in the future. We are constantly making choices today that will create new "oughts" and "have tos" in our life tomorrow. We may not be able to change the commitments we made yesterday, but we can think about the implications of the choices and decisions we will make today and tomorrow.

Spiritual Disciplines That Link Faith and Economics

If our religious commitments are to be more than a Sunday-morning affair, we need to find ways to link what happens on Sunday morning with the rest of our life. Spiritual disciplines are activities designed to integrate religion into the whole of our lives. Some of the traditional spiritual disciplines can be used in ways that focus on the link between economic life, economic justice, and faith.

Prayer

Prayer is perhaps the most fundamental daily discipline for Christians. For many, it is also the hardest to pursue regularly. We live activity-filled lives, with too little time to be alone or quiet. For prayer to become a daily part of our lives, it must be a discipline, something that we do regularly, regardless of the day's schedule or our mood or the demands of our family or job. Daily prayer is like regular family communication. There are times when we feel like doing it, times when it is convenient, and times when it is not. But being faithful in prayer deepens and builds a relationship between us and God, like that which is built when marriage partners work at keeping in touch with each other's needs and concerns.

If we are to connect economic concerns and religious concerns, our prayers must reflect that connection. Prayer is an activity that both wrestles with the uncertainties and pain of life, and celebrates the gifts of life. Thus, we can use prayer as a time when we struggle with such diverse economic questions as:

- What does God demand of my economic resources? How should I divide my income between my needs and my giving to others?

- How should I respond to those persons who ask me for money on the street?
- What is my calling? How should I deal with my current job problems? Should I take on new responsibilities at church?

Prayer can also be a time for recognizing the gifts with which our lives are currently blessed, such as:

- Thanking God for the abundance in our lives that provides us with food and shelter.
- Thanking God for the choices we have, for schooling, for jobs, for where we live, and how we live.

Prayer can involve intercession and supplication:

- For those who suffer from hunger or disease.
- For those who have no choices, whose lives are constrained by poverty or oppression.

Prayer can involve confession:

- For being too busy with our own lives and seeing too little of the pain and injustice experienced by others.
- For giving only a little of our time or a little of our money to others.
- For resisting hard choices; for ignoring those tasks that would help others but involve sacrifice on our part.

In daily prayer we can recognize our connections to the entire global community and wrestle with how to make faithful economic decisions in our own lives.

Study and Learning

The world is a complex place; we continuously face new challenges and new issues. Those who make the most of such opportunities are people who continue to learn. I recall an adult education class several years ago, in which we were discussing the pros and cons of inclusive language in worship. One member of the church, who was in his eighties, made a passionate statement at the end of one session about the beauty of the traditional language and the meaning that the familiar worship forms had for him. The next Sunday when we gathered again to continue our discussion, he made an announcement. He said he had spent much of the week thinking about the issue and had decided that he was wrong. The world was changing and he had to be open to those changes. Inclusive language was something he would try to listen to and learn from.

Just as this man was still learning and still open to new ideas, so all of us would benefit by remaining equally open to new ways of thinking. We all have much to learn about our economic life together. It is particularly important to seek out opportunities that help us understand more about how our lives are connected to those from different races, different income levels, and different countries. We must be open to understanding the lenses through which our neighbors look at the world. Such openness requires that we continue to listen to new ideas and to put ourselves in situations where we are students. By this I don't mean we all have to go back to school–there are many opportunities to be a student in all sorts of nontraditional ways.

We can participate in adult study classes in church, read newspapers and magazines, or join issues-oriented groups that provide background information on their topics of concern. We can also do some new and different things in our lives–participate in an exchange with churches from other locations, get to know a foreign visitor, take an opportunity to travel, volunteer to work as a reading tutor, serve at a local soup kitchen, or become a Big Brother or Big Sister to an inner-city child. All of these activities provide the opportunity to learn, to be a student of the wider world.

The best way to understand how our lives overlap with the lives of persons from all walks of life and from all regions of the globe is to learn more about the realities and history of those who backgrounds are different from ours. It is particularly important for middle-income American church members to find ways to be in touch with those who do not experience the material abundance many Americans take for granted. The church can be a useful place to start making contacts–with other local churches whose members come from different racial, ethnic, or income backgrounds, or with missionaries and persons who have traveled abroad. It is difficult to understand problems of hunger, poverty, or discrimination without listening to those who have experienced them first-hand.

Giving Money

In his much-read book, *Spiritual Disciplines,* Richard Foster lists tithing as a form of spiritual discipline. Few things connect our economic lives and our religious lives as intimately as our decisions about what to give and where to give.

First, we face a decision about how much to spend on our own or our families' needs and how much to give away. Second, we face a decision about where to give our money: the local church? community assistance organizations? political organizations that work for change? international mission and relief efforts?

There is no simple answer to the question "How much should I give?" Each person must find an answer that feels right for him- or herself. There are times in our lives when we face heavier personal financial commitments–for our own or our children's education, for healthcare, for elderly parents, to invest in the house where we will live for many years, and so on. These are important commitments, and we should not chastise ourselves if our outside giving is necessarily less at times because of them.

On the other hand, we are all clearly called to ask of ourselves regularly, "Do I spend too much on my own personal comforts and desires and give too little away?" It is an interesting fact that low-income families give away a higher percentage of their income for charitable purposes than do higher-income families. I have worked as a volunteer soliciting donations for community causes in public areas. I know from experience that I almost never receive a donation from men or women in business suits, but am much more likely to get something from persons in work clothes.

Tithing–traditionally considered the commitment of 10 percent of one's income to the church–is not a popular concept in most churches. How recently has your pastor preached on the necessity of tithing? And what would most church members do if she or he did? We have perhaps been too ready to avoid this concept in our American churches. It is true that a 10 percent tithe would require serious budget planning for many American families. It is also true that many American families can afford such a tithe, if they consider charitable giving a major priority. In reality, most of our church members give less than 1 percent of their income to the church. In some sense, the church has not demanded enough of its members. It has not demanded that they commit the whole of their lives. It has asked only for Sunday mornings and minimal financial commitments.

It is often useful to think consciously about how much of your income you want to give over the year for charitable purposes. Few families have so much income that they do not need to do some explicit budget planning. And budgeting one's giving to others is as important as budgeting one's personal expenditures.

Deciding where to make charitable donations is often more difficult than deciding how much to give. There are a great many worthwhile organizations and causes in the world. The local church needs your support, but so does the United Way, Church World Service, and the local homeless shelter. Individuals have to decide for themselves which organizations they feel most connected to and concerned about. There is no reason to feel guilty about throwing away funding appeals if you give regularly to other organizations. Some persons will want to centralize their charitable giving in one or two places; others will write many checks.

I often have difficulty with these decisions. On the one hand, I want to provide strong support to my local church; on the other hand, there are a variety of other organizations I want to give to as well. I have typically resolved this by giving half of my tithe to the church and dividing the other half between other organizations. I still throw away each month at least a dozen solicitations from worthy organizations.

Each of us can necessarily do only a limited amount in the way of giving. In assessing our level of giving, we must find a balance between two tensions: On the one hand, we must regularly ask, "Am I giving enough? Does my checkbook reflect my Christian commitments?" On the other hand, we must recognize our limits and not be overcome by guilt about the things we cannot do. The Lord will recognize our efforts when we make them in good faith.

Living the Life of a Christian

Although our monetary commitments are important, they are not the only measure of our concern for our neighbor. To commit our heart, we must give with our hands as well as our pocketbook. Our personal lifestyle involves many things. It involves the issues discussed above–prayer, study, and giving. It also involves the way we treat our neighbors– our family, our actual next-door neighbors, and our far-away global neighbors. But there are at least three additional ways in which individual lifestyles can demonstrate an active concern about economic injustice and the well-being of others.

Personal consumer choices. Our economic choices reflect our larger priorities. Decisions about what to buy, where to work, and where to live define who we are and the direction in which our life moves.

On a daily and weekly basis, we make many consumer choices, few of which we think about consciously. We are creatures of habit; our purchases look quite similar over time as we make trips to the grocery store, variety store, and local mall. Being more conscious about our consumer choices requires breaking some of these habits. It requires occasional conscious thinking about a few of the numerous small purchases that we make each week.

To be an informed and concerned consumer is not necessarily easy. There are hundreds of products on the shelves of our local grocery store among which we must choose. To avoid buying simply by habit, we need information about particular companies or products that we might want to support or avoid. Many church-related organizations or consumer advocacy groups are good sources of information about particular products. For instance, many church members in past years have boycotted Nestle products to protest their marketing techniques for infant formula, or have supported the farm worker boycott of California grapes. I have been involved with several social action committees that regularly included consumer information in the church bulletin for the use of church members.

It is important to be aware of the environmental impact

of our individual actions as well. More and more cities provide recycling locations where one can bring newspapers, aluminum, or glass. Many people actively seek out recyclable or reusable products in their shopping. Others try to curtail their energy consumption by using public transportation or limiting their use of electric appliances.

Few persons either desire or are able to change their consumer habits quickly. Becoming a more responsible consumer does not mean worrying about every product you buy on every trip to the store. It does mean deciding which issues matter to you and accommodating your lifestyle to a greater awareness of those issues. Some persons are most concerned with environmental justice and may want to focus on lifestyle changes that reflect that concern. Others are interested in community issues and might want to be more conscious about buying from local stores that support certain community efforts. Still others are concerned about Central American development and may want to inform themselves about products from Central America and the companies that do business there. No one can or should take on everything at once, but adopting even one or two small changes in lifestyle can be a way of reinforcing and reminding ourselves of the interrelatedness of our economic lives with the lives of persons everywhere.

I have a friend who works with an environmental research firm. As a result, she receives information each year on environmental violations by U.S. companies. One of her personal disciplines is to avoid purchasing products over the year from the top two or three worst offenders on this list. In addition, she often writes letters to the presidents of these companies, expressing her concern. She does this on her own. My friend has no expectation that such personal discipline will change the world, but it is a way by which she reminds herself that she is part of a larger and inter-connected world and that her actions must reflect her concerns for that world.

Voluntary involvement in service organizations. When entering the White House on the visitor's tour, one can see a quote from George Bush on the wall that reads, "From now on in America, any definition of a successful life must include serving others." It is a sentiment with which few Christians can disagree.

Personal involvement in the lives of other persons is a necessary part of a whole and faithful life. Sometimes our personal time may be consumed by the needs of family and friends. There is surely nothing unfaithful about spending one's spare time being a listener and a support to friends in need. However, there are new opportunities for understanding when we put ourselves in situations where we can become acquainted with others whom we may not meet in our normal round of activities.

Volunteer service can include everything from volunteering at the local hospital, to working as a literacy volunteer, to helping deliver Meals on Wheels for the elderly, to helping Habitat for Humanity build low-income housing. All of these situations provide an opportunity to become involved in the lives of others and to learn more about their personal and economic story. Two things can happen to you in such a setting. First, you are able to use some of your particular talents and energy to help others. Second, you have a chance to meet, befriend, and listen to persons whose lives may be very different from your own. In other words, volunteering is more than something we do to help others. It is something that we benefit from. By opening ourselves to others, we gain a greater sympathy and a greater understanding about their perspectives and problems. We expand our horizons and our compassion.

Citizen action. Direct service to others can be deeply rewarding, but there is also a need for involvement at a broader level within the community and the nation. By acting as a concerned citizen, expressing opinions, and lobbying decision makers at the local and national levels, we can influence policies that will affect the lives of many more than we can reach through personal service.

For instance, many individuals in low-income neighborhoods have been empowered through community organizing efforts aimed at reducing crime, improving city services, or cleaning up neighborhoods. Organized and cohesive action on the part of citizens and community organizations in one poor neighborhood in Trenton, New Jersey, resulted in new street lights, better trash removal, and greater police surveillance. Such efforts require both a willingness by individuals to work toward change as well as a willingness by an entire neighborhood to exercise political power and demand attention from city hall.

Citizen action is almost impossible to undertake alone. One needs to be informed about a wide range of current political issues, and political lobbying is typically most effective when it is engaged in by a group of persons. Therefore, a wide variety of citizen action groups have sprung up. At the national and international levels groups such as SANE/Freeze, Bread for the World, Interfaith Impact for Justice and Peace, and Amnesty International send regular newsletters to their members, discussing issues of public concern. Such groups also assist local groups to organize for local educational events, letter-writing campaigns, and other forms of issue lobbying. There are similar groups at the local and state levels, focusing on specific regional concerns.

Those who have not been involved in citizen activities often feel intimidated by the process: How can I write a letter to my senator? Why would anyone at city hall listen to me? That is why joining together with a larger group of people on an issue of particular concern is useful. A larger group makes background information available and provides the support and help necessary to embark on a new activity. Very few persons actually take the time to write letters or express opinions to elected representatives. As a result, even a few citizens' letters on an issue that is not currently in the media (such as U.S. aid to developing countries) attract attention in the politician's offices. This kind of such action can matter. Ask any group that has been involved in such lobbying about their successes.

Where Do I Start?

This chapter has laid out a wide variety of activities and has enthusiastically urged persons to get involved. You might have the impression that you should jump into everything at once. In reality, this is not the way to start. No one can do it all. All of us realistically face limits on our time, our energy, and our commitments.

Particularly on issues involving economic justice and the distribution of economic resources, the prospects for personal involvement can seem daunting. What can any one person do to ease the pain of 650 million hungry persons in the world? How can any of us even cope with the 33 million poor persons in the United States?

It is crucial to realize that none of us are called to *solve* any of these problems. We are called to be aware of them and do what we can to limit the economic pain in this world to the best of our ability. This typically means embarking on a limited set of activities in areas where we have something to contribute. "How can I do all this?" is the wrong question. The right question is "What can I do to make some difference right now?" Here are three suggestions:

1. For this year, pick at least one lifestyle change that you know you can handle. Such a change may involve recycling your newspapers and glass bottles, increasing your giving to the local AIDS clinic, volunteering once a month in a local Big Sister program, or joining the group fighting drugs in your neighborhood. Your action may be a much more radical one: a decision to change jobs or to leave paid employment and spend a year volunteering in an effort you care a great deal about. It doesn't matter *what* you do; it matters that you find something you would like to change about your current lifestyle, and *do* it.

2. Pick one community, national, or global issue that engages your concern as a global neighbor and that you want to understand more about. Perhaps the issue is a problem in your local schools. Perhaps it is homelessness. It could be the current famine in the Sudan. It could be the problems faced by Hispanic immigrants.

With this concern in mind, commit yourself to two things: First, seek more knowledge. Contact people and organizations working on this issue and ask for information. Read any newspaper or magazine articles on the subject that you come across. Go to the local library and ask for books.

Over a period of a few months, actively try to learn more about this issue.

Second, find a way to be involved with the issue. This may mean joining a citizen advocacy group in their efforts. It may mean simply writing a letter to your mayor, expressing your concern about this issue. It may mean getting involved in a community group that is trying to help persons faced with this problem. Involvement can be as little as writing a single letter or as much as volunteering for weekly literacy training with Hispanic immigrants who don't speak English. Again, the point is not how much you do, but that you make a start at doing something.

It is almost impossible to take on a number of different issues at once. Specialization is necessary. Take one topic, learn something about it, and get involved. It doesn't matter whether the topic is environmentally safe local waste disposal, crime in your local community, health care for the poor, or limits on nuclear weapons. Pick one issue you are concerned about. Don't feel guilty about saying no to the many solicitations for money, time, and attention from other causes. Just do what you can on the issue you've chosen.

3. Actively seek support for your efforts. On the one hand, this means seeking God's support and guidance, through prayer and worship. It also means finding other persons who share your concern. In your church, in your neighborhood, or through existing organizations, find others to talk with, to share information with, and to work with. Few of us can work on justice issues by ourselves. We need a broader community. The church, as a community of faithful and committed persons, is often crucial in providing this type of support and assistance.

Ultimately, we must think about *transforming* our lives. This is not an easy task to accomplish. Very few persons have conversion experiences that change them forever. Most of us struggle along, making small changes here and there in our lifestyles and our behavior, backsliding, and then trying again. Yet in the end, it is those small changes that are exactly what transformation is all about. Faithfulness to

God is not demonstrated through grand gestures, but through faithfulness in the small and mundane details of living. Small steps are a sufficient beginning.

Fortunately, we are not alone in this effort. The Holy Spirit is present in the world. We do not transform our lives through our own power; rather, our lives are transformed by the power of the Holy Spirit. You will need to seek the help and the presence of the Spirit as you seek to make changes in your life.

Summary

If we are to integrate our economic and our faith lives, we must look at the choices that we make in our personal lives and ask how they reflect our concern for God's far-flung household. Such a commitment requires regular prayer, allowing us to confess our failings and renew our commitments. It requires an ongoing openness to learn new things, to put ourselves in new situations, and to meet people from other backgrounds. It requires us to be faithful stewards of our money, explicitly deciding how much we will give to others. It means finding ways in which our daily activities reflect our commitment to economic justice and our concern about the economic pain of others. Thus we may consciously examine our economic decisions and lifestyles, give time to volunteer activities, and become involved in citizen action. By picking a few activities and issues with which we are particularly concerned and focusing our energy on learning more and doing more on these specific issues, we can make a difference in our own lives and in the lives of others around us.

GROUP DISCUSSION AND ACTIVITIES

Suggested Group Exercise

Give each individual a sheet of paper. Ask everyone to list six categories down the left side of the paper: Prayer and Worship;   Study and Learning;   Personal Giving;   Personal Lifestyle; Volunteer Activities; and Citizen Action. Ask participants to list under each category anything in these areas that they have done over the past year that relates their faith to the economic world around them. After everyone has done this, develop together a "master chart" for the group. You might be surprised at the range of activities within the group. Discuss any possible actions not on the chart that members of the group have considered or think might be possible.

Starting Discussion Questions

1. What aspects of your economic life seem like economic choices? Which ones seem like "musts" or "oughts"?

2. How do you make decisions in your life about how much to give? Is this a conscious budget decision, or is it the result of how much money is left after all other bills have been paid? How do you choose among organizations to give to? What solicitations do you throw away? Which ones do you read? How do you decide?

3. Invite someone in your church who is involved politically to talk about instances when he or she has been involved in citizen action, or instances when he or she has seen citizen activities influence public policy makers.

4. Women have traditionally done a great deal of volunteer work, but as more and more women have entered the paid labor force, volunteering has declined in this country. Is this good or bad? How can organizations (such as the church) that have often relied heavily upon volunteer work adjust to this change?

5. What (if any) lifestyle changes have you made in your life in recent years by choice (for example, to exercise more, recycle, eat less fat or cholesterol, engage regularly in meditation or prayer, and so on.) How hard were these changes? What helped you make them? What advice would you give someone who wanted to make lifestyle changes because of his or her faith commitments?

CHAPTER 8
The Economic Life of the Church

As Christians, we are more than individuals acting alone in the world. We are part of a local church, and through that, part of the worldwide Christian church with all of its varieties and denominations. Just as we are called as individuals to integrate our personal economic and religious lives, so the church also must face decisions about how to act as a church institution in the economic world. Churches that issue bold pronouncements about economic justice must be willing to look at economic justice issues within their own institutions.

The Church and the Individual

How do the church's activities overlap with those of individual Christians as discussed in the preceding chapter? First, the church must provide the support and resources necessary for individuals to grow in faith, to transform their lives, and to better integrate their weekly activities with their Sunday morning worship. The church should provide a worshiping community that recognizes the interconnections between religious faith and all aspects of individual life, one that helps individuals struggle with how to make those connections in their own lives.

Chapter 7 noted the importance of community support for individuals struggling to adopt faithful economic lifestyles or working on issues of economic justice. The church is an institution in which individuals should be able to find strength to face economic pain in their own lives or empowerment to struggle against economic injustice.

Second, the church–in all of its manifestations–is more than a place where individuals come together. It is a major social institution, existing independently of the political and secular organizations in the community and in the nation. As such, it can play a role in raising the visibility of economic justice issues in the larger society. There are at least two public roles for the church. On the one hand, it can and should speak out publicly, condemning poverty, seeking peace, and speaking for the oppressed. On the other hand, the church can do more than speak. For the church to have credibility when it speaks against economic injustice, it must address inequities and injustices within its own institutional structure. It must structure itself as a role model to secular society.

Particularly for those of us who belong to churches that encourage broad membership participation, if we believe that God calls us to act against injustice and to be concerned with the well-being of our neighbors in all places, there is a responsibility to see that our church–locally and nationally–also acts against injustice and for peace. For instance, the United Church of Christ is based on a congregational polity. All members have a vote at their local church's congregational meeting, which is the ultimate source of decision-making authority. Thus, the local church is not a mysterious institution controlled by unknown powers. The church is *our* organization, whose direction and activities we control.

Worship Activities

The primary role of the local church is to be a place of common worship, where all people come together to pray, to celebrate, to worship, and to learn more about the God who rules our lives. There are many aspects to public worship. One of the most fundamental is that public worship is a place where people come to find God–to seek God's presence and support and to learn more of God's intentions for each person's life.

Worship should recognize God's concern with the economic well-being of all of God's household. Public worship should thus regularly involve

• Confession of our inattention to economic injustices and our involvement in the structures that exclude and oppress others in the world around us.

- Recognition, in all aspects of worship, of our interconnectedness to all of humanity.
- Recognition of God's concern for the whole of our lives and the linkages between our Sunday worship behavior and our individual choices and dilemmas throughout the week.
- Teaching about God's concern for the poor and God's concern with economic justice, interpreted in ways that have meaning for our modern lives.

These issues can be raised through prayer, preaching, confession, music, biblical readings, and bulletin announcements. In short, all aspects of worship can be used to reflect these concerns.

There are, of course, many other important and vital aspects of public worship. Services that focus only and always on issues of economic justice fail to provide attention and support for the many other demands in a worship service. The question is one of balance. Economic justice issues should not be shunned in public worship, nor should they be the primary and central aspect of each Sunday's worship concern. Rather, they should be a regularly recognized theme in a church's worship program.

There is another important aspect of the church's worship life that is too often considered peripheral to worship. The worship service regularly includes an offering, a time for individuals to give monetary gifts for the ongoing work of the church. As discussed in the previous chapter, a personal decision about giving money is as much a religious issue as a personal decision about which church to join. The church has a responsibility to talk openly about money issues as an aspect of Christian life. Discussing budgets or asking for money for local church efforts or for outreach and mission should not be an embarrassing activity.

Through its collection of offerings the church provides channels for Christians to engage in regular tithing and giving. Special offerings often provide an opportunity to give to outreach work around the globe or to support local assistance organizations. Regular gifts to the church support the worship and educational program of the church.

Too often the offering is a part of the worship service that has little shape. Unlike the prayers or the sermons or the opening liturgy, the call to offering is often done with the same words and in the same way week after week. In ignoring the offering as a crucial part of its spiritual and teaching work, a church loses an opportunity to better address economic issues. Offerings can be combined with prayer, with congregational singing, with movement, or with personal statements of commitment and concern. Creative attention to the offering can be an important innovation in many worship services. Personal giving deserves more sustained discussion and attention in worship than it is accorded once a year on Stewardship Sunday.

Educational Activities

A vital part of the church's role is its educational program. For children, the Sunday school provides an arena in which to learn about the church and about God and to explore moral problems in their growing lives. Education is not just for children, however; all of us can continue to learn and grow in our faith. Many churches offer regular or occasional adult education programs.

Of course, a great deal of adult education occurs during the regular worship service through prayers, confession, music, and preaching. Additional educational opportunities also abound within most churches. Regular church newsletters can be the source of articles on social outreach, community needs, and economic concerns. Bulletin boards and in-church announcements often alert people to current economic and social issues. One-on-one conversations with other church members provide perhaps the most effective form of communication. During coffee hour after the service is when I most regularly learn about the concerns of other members. Once a month, at coffee hour, the Social Action Committee in a church of which I was once a member set up a table with resources focusing on a particular issue, such as local race relations, domestic poverty, community needs for low-income housing, or the AIDS epidemic. Members of the church who were familiar with the particular issue were available to talk to those who wanted to learn more.

Even with all of these informal channels of education in the church, there is always room for formal educational events. Among the ideas for adult education hours that can work effectively are the following:

- Bible study, focusing on "What does the Bible say about economics?"
- Visitors from overseas, discussing the problems of another country or another people, and the connection of those problems with U.S. economic and government policies.
- Sessions focused on personal giving, tithing, socially responsible investing, bequests, and so forth.
- After-church field trips, visits to churches or neighborhoods in other areas of the local community or to a local homeless shelter or food bank.
- Events that give members a chance to talk with and listen to those from other cultures, other races, and other economic backgrounds.

The local church can provide the educational opportunities that help their members link faith issues to justice, peace, environmental, and lifestyle issues.

The Institutional Lifestyle of the Local Church

The local church, like most families, has a budget. It raises money, it spends money, it pays salaries, and it buys materials. Just as we are personally called to be conscious of whether our personal lifestyles mesh with our Christian commitments, so also should each local church be concerned that its institutional lifestyle and its budget reflect its mission. It is worth asking yourself the question "If I look at my local church budget, can I tell that it is a church budget rather than the budget of any other community organization?"

One activity that local churches may find useful is to undertake an economic audit of the church, analyzing where the church's money is going and how well the budget reflects the church's sense of its own mission. There are a number of issues on which such an audit might want to focus.

The employees of the church. We have discussed certain types of economic injustices in the labor market: lack of health insurance, jobs that demand too much and pay too little, and discrimination against women, older workers, and minority workers. These are easy to condemn in general, but too many local churches have engaged in just such practices. I have been part of local churches that did not pay health insurance for the maintenance staff, that paid astonishingly low wages to the secretarial staff, and that paid ministerial salaries well below those of most church members. I have also been part of local churches that were struggling to correct these problems. For instance, I know of one church that froze virtually all other aspects of its budget for two years until it could afford to provide health insurance for its maintenance and clerical staff.

Church purchasing. Churches buy many things, including Sunday school materials, cleaning supplies, and office equipment. From whom does your church buy these? Some churches have stopped using Styrofoam cups and now use more recyclable products during coffee hour (even, sometimes, the old china cups). One church intentionally patronizes an office equipment and supply store that is run by a person who donates a large amount of money to local community organizations. Another church has recently started purchasing its paper supplies from a local minority-owned business located in a neighborhood in need of renewal and jobs. All of these are conscious lifestyle decisions for the church.

Outreach. Churches have institutional responsibilities to their employees, to their buildings, and to their programs. Budgets are always limited, and it is always difficult to decide how much money goes where. Just as Christian families are called to ask, "Am I giving enough?" so local churches should constantly face the question "Are we doing enough for outreach, missions, and our neighbors outside our walls?"

As institutions become established, they often lose their original sense of mission and focus increasingly on rituals, buildings, and personalities. The winds of reform have regularly swept through Christianity, calling it away from an overemphasis on the material rewards of this world and back to an emphasis on God. Local churches have to be constantly alert to the temptation to expand their own comforts and forget broader issues. Attention to cushions and carpets should not replace attention to the larger mission of the church.

Small churches often face substantial fixed costs. They must pay a pastor and keep up a building. Few small churches can give more than 12 to 15 percent of their budget to outside missions, but many larger churches can do better. Many large churches work hard to assure that 20 to 25 percent or more of their budget is shared with others and allocated to organizations, activities, and needs outside their own church congregation. If your church budget for sharing is well below these figures, it may be time to think hard about your church priorities.

Churches with the wealth to maintain some endowment funds or savings have special opportunities and special responsibilities. The church is not a business corporation, and the sole mission of a church endowment fund should not be to maximize financial return. Endowments should be used wisely, and sometimes this means they should be spent rather than saved. One church, after much debate, decided to invest half of its endowment in the first major effort at low-income housing development in their community. The risks in this endeavor were much higher than if that money had stayed in a money market fund. But the members decided that their mission as a church demanded that they take these risks. Over five years, they realized a lower return on that money than a money market fund would have provided. Instead, they supported an important community effort that successfully improved housing opportunities for a number of low-income families in their town.

Investment decisions are also economic choices that should reflect the mission of the church. More and more churches are actively involved in socially responsible investing. Many churches avoid companies that are involved in nuclear weapons production, companies that have not complied with specific guidelines for doing business in South Africa, companies that are cited for major environmental damage, or companies involved in particularly vicious labor disputes. Groups such as the Interfaith Center for Corporate Responsibility can provide information to churches on how to become involved in socially responsible investing.

An economic audit of a church may cover many issues other than those listed here. It can include a review of the entire worship and educational program of the church. It may usefully include some all-church discussion of the local church's priorities and sense of mission. In short, it is a way for a church to assess where it is now, where it is going, and the choices it has made and wants to make in the future. Like our family budget, our church budget reflects who we are and who we want to be.

Community Involvement and Political Activity

Perhaps the most intense debate in American religion over in the past few decades has been over the role of the church in the larger political realm. Does the church have the right to challenge the state? To protest government policies? To lobby for specific legislation? To endorse candidates?

Our religious heritage provides many examples of faithful people called to challenge the current political structure. Prophets have continually emerged at crucial points in history and have preached and acted against the distribution of wealth and power in society (often to the discomfort of the official church structure). Moses did so, as did Isaiah, John Calvin, and Martin Luther King Jr. Jesus was killed, not just because of his religious teachings, but also because he was a threat to the political establishment of his day.

Historically, the American church has been deeply involved in political questions. The Episcopal church was the official state church of Virginia for many years. The Congregational church was a leading advocate of abolition, and many members of that church engaged in civil disobedience to protest slavery. Quakers have supported conscientious dissent from the military since the beginning of the American state, and both sides in the current debate over abortion claim connections with the church.

Our Christian heritage demands that we apply Christian teachings to our modern life. If there is no way to divorce religious practice from daily life, then religion and politics are inevitably connected. The famous statement by Karl Barth echoes in our present time: A Christian must face the world with the Bible in one hand and the newspaper in the other.

This view does not threaten the separation of church and state as embodied in the U.S. constitution. Such a separation was never meant to imply that the church should remain uninvolved in political affairs, only that the church and state should never be combined in one institution, as occurs when a "state church" is recognized and supported. The state–the local city hall, the state department of transportation, or the U.S. Supreme Court–is a collection of secular institutions. The church is not. It speaks out of a particular moral stance, shaped by its religious tradition. It has every right to speak publicly on issues.

In fact, it is the very independence of the church that gives it moral authority in the public realm. The church is not the instrument of any particular political party or lobby group. Its loyalty is to a larger and more universal perspective. As such, the church has a different viewpoint from most secular organizations. When operating at its best, the church can speak for groups that are often voiceless or concerns that are often unheard in the political process– for the poor of other lands, for the poor of this nation, against the long-term danger of environmental destruction, or for the vision of universal peace.

Thus, it is not just individual church members who can become involved in political concerns. The church as an institution has a role to play in local and national political affairs. The church can operate as a voice of conscience and a voice of prophecy. It can ask the uncomfortable question "What does this do for the poor?" which so often goes unasked.

A local church can get involved in politics, both through the involvements of its individual members and as a local institution. I have testified at a zoning commission hearing on behalf of my local church, supporting a plan to increase low-income housing. I have attended a city council meeting as a representative of my church to support the establishment of a local shelter for the homeless. In these cases, my own power as a citizen was strengthened because I spoke not just for myself but had been authorized by my local church to speak for that entire institution. Similarly, churches that I have attended have passed resolutions supporting international arms negotiation, have sent protests to the president about cutbacks in aid to the poor, and have sent petitions to the mayor to improve services in poor neighborhoods.

These efforts on the part of local churches inevitably involve debate and discussion. A local church can validly speak in a public arena only when it has achieved broad internal consensus. Some churches have members who are basically in agreement on social issues and it is relatively easy for them to act as a church institution. On issues about which there is intense internal disagreement among the church membership, it may not be possible for the church to speak institutionally. In these cases, the primary role for the church may be to provide a forum for discussion, debate, and education on the issues.

It is important to recognize that discussion and education do not inevitably lead to agreement. A church can openly discuss political issues only if everyone agrees to respect opposing opinions. Any church that undertakes a serious study of the linkages between religious, economic, and political life must be willing to deal with internal disagreement. A church community must have enough trust between its members that they can disagree without developing personal animosity. Some of my most fruitful discussions have been with fellow church members whose political viewpoints were quite different from my own. I have learned from them, occasionally I have changed my mind, occasionally they have changed their minds, and often we have agreed to disagree. Whatever the outcome, I left the conversation with a better understanding of their points of view.

The church is an institution that is both of this world and not of this world. As such, it is called to prophesy, to speak as a moral voice in the current political realm. Those of us who are active in local churches must see that the church carries out this responsibility. Yet, there are dangers in such action. The church is a humanly constructed organization that can become too easily caught in the web of power, status, and publicity that surrounds public issues. A church that ventures into the public realm is always at risk of losing its moral authority by becoming caught up in the same political power struggles faced by secular institutions.

Maintaining an independent and open perspective on public issues will always be a challenge. The church must speak for the right as it interprets the right. All of our past history, however, warns us against moral certainty. Even as the church speaks as an institution, it must remain open to other voices and other opinions. It must always be willing to admit voices of dissent and listen to those who would interpret the church's mission in other ways. Fear of being wrong should not be paralyzing; the church must act in this world. It must find a way to do this with humility and openness. In the quest for the right, it must avoid the smug certainty of righteousness.

Beyond the Local Church

Whereas most church members are primarily involved in their local church and its activities, the larger regional and national bodies of the church are also important actors in the church's role in public affairs. Regional and national agencies offer support to local churches on education programs. National agencies and interfaith groups coordinate and support mission projects. National and regional leaders–district and regional ministers, national agency leaders, and denominational presidents–also speak publicly for the church in many forums. The linkage between economic life and Christian faith can be strengthened by the work of these larger bodies.

Regional associations and national agencies of the church. These groups often sponsor educational events, provide support and training for local church personnel, and coordinate multichurch efforts. It is important that local churches demand that such groups pay attention to the issues of economic justice and to the links between economic and faith issues. For instance, educational materials need to be available supporting Bible study and discussion of economic justice issues. Regional conferences on these issues can provide opportunities for people from a variety of churches to share their ideas and concerns.

National agencies typically coordinate both the direct mission outreach of the church and its political activities. Many denominations join together in these efforts. Thus, Church World Service is supported by a broad range of denominations in its fund-raising and foreign outreach work. Interfaith Impact for Justice and Peace does both issues analysis and lobbying in Washington for all of its member denominations. A number of denominations also have their own staff members in Washington, D.C., and coordinate their work with each other to cover a range of legislative issues. It is important that these organizations maintain contact with local congregations and church members, educating them about these national efforts and encouraging their participation and involvement.

The economic lifestyle of the larger church. Like local churches facing many economic choices, so our regional and national church bodies must be faithful in their use of money. The budgets and the work of larger church bodies can benefit from the same sort of economic audit discussed for the local church. In addition to the standard set of budget decisions, the national church also faces a variety of difficult distributional choices. How much money should rich churches be required to share with poorer churches? How much inequity in ministerial salaries should occur across churches? How much should national agency personnel be paid? These are often divisive issues within the church. At the same time, they are issues that directly reflect a church's commitments. A church that preaches greater economic equality for the wider society should be willing to practice greater equality in its own institutional arrangements.

Seminaries. The leadership of the church is trained in seminary to do the work of the church. Very few seminaries at present offer opportunities for their students to learn more about the interactions between economic life and faith. Seminaries should be encouraged to increase their offerings of courses that provide a framework for linking these issues, for thinking about economic issues in the church, and for analyzing public policy issues.

Cross-church and international connections. The universal and diverse nature of the Christian church provides a unique opportunity for Christians to come into contact with persons from many economic, racial, and cultural backgrounds. Too often, both local churches and larger church denominations limit their contacts to other churches much like their own. Through the larger church, however, there is a unique opportunity for individuals to have contact with persons from across the world.

The church is one of the few institutions that can speak with a global perspective. Even those denominations that are solely based in the United States have global connections. They operate international mission projects, they are united with sister churches in other countries, and they preach a gospel of the common humanity of all peoples. This aspect of the church is often underappreciated and underutilized. American churches in particular have often been guilty of a traditional missions perspective in which they ask only, "What can we do for the poor of the world?" We need to ask that question, but we also need to ask, "What can we learn from churches and Christians in other parts of the world?" In other words, we need to ask how other churches can help us expand our global perspective.

Churches in other countries are publicly struggling with oppression, economic inequities, and social injustice. Out of this struggle, they provide international leadership on issues of economic life and Christian faith. Listening to these voices, to their stories, and to what they have learned from their experiences is a necessary exercise for the American church. It is because of these international, cross-racial, and crosscultural connections that the church can play a truly unique role in both national and global politics.

Summary

The church is the center of religious life for most Christians. Local churches must provide support for individuals who seek to meld their economic and religious lives. Churches can address issues of economic justice and economic life through worship activities and through education programs. But the local church is also an important role model for economic equity. An economic audit of local churches is a way to review budgets and spending priorities and to focus on the institutional lifestyle of the church.

Both locally and nationally, the church is also called to engage in efforts to increase economic justice, to provide a voice for the perspectives and opinions of the poor and the oppressed. This public role requires debate, discussion, and education within the church. Sometimes this activity will lead to a consensus, other times it will not. The church must be careful when it enters the public realm that it remains an open and inclusive organization. Regional and national church bodies play an important role in supporting local churches and in coordinating the church's actions in national and international affairs. The church is also an international institution that crosses boundaries of nationality, race, and culture. This provides the church with an international perspective. American churches may find these connections particularly useful to learn more about the realities facing others around the globe.

GROUP DISCUSSION AND ACTIVITIES

Suggested Group Exercise

Divide participants into four small groups. Assign each group one of the following categories: Worship and education activities of our local church; Institutional lifestyle and budget of our local church; Activities of our regional and national church bodies; and Public involvement of the local and national church in political activities. Have members of each group first list, for their assigned category, all the instances they know in which the church addresses issues of economics and economic justice through these activities. Second, have each group brainstorm about new ways that the church could use these activities to address economic issues. After the small groups have completed their discussions, reassemble together in the original group and create a large matrix of current and possible activities for the church.

Starting Discussion Questions

1. How does your church present its offering each week? Brainstorm about alternative ways to introduce or collect the offering that might get the congregation thinking in new ways about personal giving.

2. What is your local church's commitment to outreach and giving? Is this adequate? If you wanted to increase the amount, what trade-offs would you have to make with other budget categories?

3. How well does your local church deal with its employees? Many people argue that those who work for the church should willingly accept lower salaries, because that is part of their commitment to God. Others argue that salaries in the church should be based on need rather than on experience or education (that is, the church should provide an alternative economic model to society). Do you agree with either of these perspectives?

4. Indicate examples (historical or current) in which the church has spoken publicly on political issues in ways that you thought were helpful. Indicate examples of instances when you think the church might have taken an inappropriate public stand. Give examples of occasions when you think the church should have spoken publicly, but remained silent. What are the differences between these situations?

5. How much sharing occurs between poorer and wealthier churches in your denomination? What are the advantages and disadvantages of redistributing resources between churches?

CHAPTER 9

Public Policy: Is There a Christian Perspective?

The last two chapters argued that both individuals and the church as an institution should be involved with public policy issues, through education-related activities as well as lobbying and public statements. How do individuals or the church take up this task? In particular, how do they decide which issues they will speak for and which ones they will speak against? This chapter addresses these questions, exploring ways to approach public policy issues from a faith-based perspective.

Interpreting the Signs of Our Times

The primary source of authority for Christians is the Bible. This is a book that contains an astonishing amount of wisdom; it is a wonderful source of information about how to understand ourselves and our relation to God and our neighbor. But there are some things that the Bible cannot do. In particular, the Bible cannot tell us exactly how to act in many modern situations. It can provide guiding principles for our actions, but the translation of those principles into the specific behaviors we choose is often a matter of our own judgment. The Bible tells us to give to the poor. Does this mean we must give money to every individual in need we see on the street? Or can we support the local homeless shelter and not respond to individuals who ask for assistance personally? Each individual Christian must decide how much he or she will give and in what ways.

Similarly, the Bible provides guiding principles for our social and political life together. The "marks of a just economy" presented in chapter 4 provide one set of guiding principles based on the biblical discussion of economics and economic justice. It is up to us as individuals and as a community to decide how we will organize our common life to meet these demands. The Bible tells us that all should be included in the economy and the household of God. We interpret this to mean that all persons should have access to food and shelter, but the Bible does not tell us whether the best way to do this is to run a food stamp program or to create public sector jobs. It does not tell us whether we should build public housing or provide income supplements to low-income families.

In the end, we must interpret the signs of our times. We must use our own limited wisdom to decide how to act as faithful Christians in making policy choices.

Acting with Discernment

Deciding which public policies will lead to a more just and equitable economy is not an easy task. It takes prayer, study, experience, wisdom, and perhaps a bit of foolhardiness. There are at least three things to keep in mind:

First, good judgment often requires more than faith. Although a commitment to help and serve others is a vital part of the Christian faith, in and of itself it may not be enough to discern adequately the appropriate direction for action. Good intentions do not always produce good ethical choices. Public action requires *both* prayer and study. Questions such as "How can we effectively reduce poverty in this country?" pose difficult problems, and a wise answer requires experience and understanding of the conditions and causes underlying poverty in the United States today. It is also important to recognize that "wisdom" is not the same as "many years of education." We can acquire wisdom about poverty by working and talking with the poor, by seeking out others whose opinions we trust, as well as by reading and studying in more traditional ways.

Second, it is important to recognize that faithful people can disagree about the details of how to design good public policies. Even after all of us agree on the need to eliminate homelessness in this country, we can still disagree on the best way to go about doing that. This should induce humility about the positions we choose to support, as well as an openness to listen to those with whom we disagree. God tells us to care for the poor among us, yet God does not tell us precisely how to do this. It is foolishness on our part to assume that our personal wisdom is so great that only our own solution can be the right one.

Third, the need for wisdom and the always present possibility of being wrong in our judgments does not excuse us from acting in the public realm to the best of our abilities. We have choice in deciding what issues we work on, what programs we support, and how we pursue economic justice in our own lives. We have, however, no choice in whether or not we should care about these issues. That is a tenet of our faith. Even a choice to avoid such issues will inevitably affect the outcome. By choosing not to give to outreach and mission, we affect the work that outreach organizations can do. By choosing not to vote, we cede our vote and our voice to others who choose to express an opinion.

Accepting our call to be "fools for Christ" is a fundamental part of social action and outreach. We will only imperfectly understand the economic pain around us; we are human and we make mistakes. A core part of human sin is a limited ability or willingness to understand. We must confess and confront this sin, but we must not be immobilized by it. Not acting and not speaking because we are afraid of being wrong or looking foolish can also lead to sin. In the end, we must exercise our human ability of *discernment*, to decide when to speak and when to keep silent.

Choosing Our Actions

In chapter 7 we discussed the problem of feeling overwhelmed as individuals. There are so many important issues, and all of us have limited time, energy, and abilities. It is worth repeating that no one is called to do everything. Each individual must choose the issue or issues to which he or she has the most to contribute. Some persons will choose to work on changes in their own neighborhood, some on environmental justice, and some on housing. *Specialization* is necessary in the outreach work and public issues advocacy that we choose to do. Wisdom and discernment–important qualities when working in the public realm–come only with experience, time, and attention to an issue.

An Example: Policies to Address Poverty in the United States

One of the marks of a just economy stated that "a just economy gives all persons access to the basic material necessities of life." We have already discussed how inadequately the United States meets this challenge. Thirty-three million persons are poor in the United States. Some 500,000 persons are homeless. Over 5 million children in this country regularly go hungry.

We cannot remain inactive in the face of such facts. These are our neighbors, who live among us. What is the role of individual Christians and of the church in promoting public policies designed to alleviate poverty? There are at least three ways in which public activity can be directed.

Speaking Out Against Injustice

One role for the church and for individuals involved in the church is to act as the conscience of the nation, speaking out against the economic injustice of poverty. As Christians we have something to say about the dignity and value of all human beings, about the inclusiveness of our household economy, and about the meaning of justice. A major role for the prophets of the church has been to denounce injustice and oppression. In the face of poverty and need, the church can play an important public role, educating others, demanding change, and empowering the poor to speak about their pain.

Providing an Alternative Framework: Economic Rights

Our public role should not be limited merely to denouncing and criticizing current injustices. We have an alternative framework to propose. The call to include all persons in the abundance of the household is a call for *economic rights*.

This country has long led the way in implementing political rights for all of its citizens. We take it as a matter of course that each citizen should have the right to participate in the political process. Although we have not always provided this right to all groups at all times, we continue to consider it a national goal that all persons have a *voice* in public decision making.

In a similar manner, the recognition that all persons must be included in the household economy is a call to develop an inclusive economic system where all can claim access to food, shelter, education, health care, and employment. This call recognizes the rights of all persons to these basic necessities. Just as individuals have a political right to be part of the decision-making process if they choose, so also in a just economy individuals who do not have adequate resources for survival in the community have a right to claim a share of the economic resources of the larger society.

The political rights associated with citizenship also contain within them responsibilities–citizens have responsibilities to obey the laws, to respect the rights of other citizens, and to participate in the political process in an informed way. At an extreme, when an individual fundamentally violates these responsibilities (commits a felony), we remove his or her voting rights.

So, also, are economic rights attached to attendant responsibilities. An economy that grants all citizens a basic right of access to adequate health care, education, employment, housing, and food can also validly require that persons use these rights responsibly. For instance, those who attend public schools have a responsibility to obey the rules by which these schools are run, to attend classes, meet performance standards, avoid drugs and weapons in school, and so forth. Those who receive housing assistance have a responsibility to maintain that property, for their family and for those who will follow them. A person who is consistently absent from a job without good cause may forfeit the right to employment. And, perhaps most important of all, such economic rights necessarily require a commitment by taxpayers to fund the education, health, and employment systems that assure access to everyone.

If our faith commitment is to provide all human beings with the resources necessary for life, this means supporting public policies that assure adequate resources are available to those most in need. If this is a fundamental responsibility of our society, then these economic rights should be encoded into the laws of this country. The original draft of the United Church of Christ *Pronouncement* proposed amending the Constitution to include a statement of economic rights, as a way of making it clear that these are as important as the more familiar political rights. Opponents argued that a constitutional change might be too restrictive and difficult to draft and that legislative changes could be sufficient by themselves. Although the latter argument won in the final draft of the *Pronouncement*, the suggestion of a constitutional amendment makes clear what a commitment to economic justice might entail. Symbolically, it shows just how simple–and how radical–such a change would be.

Drafting Specific Policies

The third public role for the church and for church members is to be involved in the details of drafting specific policies that would assure adequate economic resources for those in need. Most denominations have staff based in Washington, D.C., who are involved in the drafting and adoption of specific policy proposals.

Decisions on which specific policy proposals to support, which compromises to work for, and which proposals to work against, are difficult to make. Neither biblical revelation nor broad guiding principles are typically very useful in determining how much funding should be provided in a welfare reform bill for job training versus child care for low-income women.

Detailed involvement in such issues is often difficult for those who do not have professional interests or training and experience in the field. This is why many education/ advocacy organizations have sprung up, providing their members with short, readable background information on the issues they address. Thus, members who are asked to write letters encouraging their senator to support a particular policy proposal are also given the information they need to understand why this proposal is advantageous.

What Would an Anti-Poverty Agenda Look Like?

Using the framework of economic rights discussed above, what changes in the current system of support for low-income individuals might be proposed? There are a wide variety of possible proposals. To give a sense of what a societal commitment to basic economic rights might mean, I discuss a few of these below.

1. Access to jobs and job training. Employment is a vital necessity for most households. Jobs not only provide necessary income, but they are also an avenue for individuals to participate in society, to interact with others, and to receive affirmation for their abilities and efforts. Over the past decade, however, between 5 to 10 percent of the labor force has been unemployed at any given time. Another substantial number have jobs, but earn too little income to support their families; 16 percent of poor families have at least one family member who works full-time year-round. One of the marks of a just economy is that it is "inclusive, involving all able people in responsible, participatory, and economically rewarding activity."

Assuring adequate jobs requires putting priority on policies that create jobs and expand employment. The policy question "What does it do for the poor?" in this case becomes "Will this policy encourage employment and jobs?" Local governments might encourage new business locations in poorer areas. State governments might strengthen state employment and training programs. The federal government might provide more extensive funds for job training or consider wage subsidies to low-wage workers. All of these policies would help move the economy toward a situation in which more low-income families are able to find self-supporting employment in the mainstream economy.

2. Health care. Over 30 million persons in this country have no health insurance. As the costs of health care continue to rise, lack of insurance means lack of access. The United States has the most inequitable system of health care among industrialized nations. Those who are fully insured often receive high quality care, but those without insurance go without care.

In recent years the federal government has legislated an expansion of Medicaid (which insures a limited number of low-income families) to include all children under the age of 5 in families below 133 percent of the poverty line. Future expansions will include older children as well. This legislation is a good example of a movement toward a more inclusive and just economic system. Other efforts to provide more comprehensive health care to all uninsured families are also needed. Many people support some form of a national health care system, such as all other industrialized nations provide.

3. Income support. Although long-run self sufficiency through employment may be a desirable goal for many poor families, there are those for whom this cannot be accomplished. The elderly or the severely disabled are not able to work. Many persons with very young children or with elderly relatives who require home care are unable to seek employment. Among all poor persons, fully 50 percent are either children, under age eighteen, or elderly, over age sixty-five. Employment cannot solve the problems of poverty for these individuals.

There must be adequate income support for those who are unable to find or hold a job. Programs providing such support, however, are quite limited in this country. A woman with two young children and no other income can expect to receive only $629 a month in income support (through welfare and food stamp programs), the equivalent of $7548 a year and well below the poverty line. This amount also varies enormously across states. Many households—single nonelderly individuals or married couples without children—have virtually no sources of temporary support if they find themselves in extreme need.

A national federal minimum for welfare payments would provide greater equity and assure all families at least a minimal support level. The value of welfare payments has fallen over the past two decades, as inflation has increased while payments levels have stayed constant. Payments should be increased and indexed to the level of inflation (as is the case with Social Security payments.) In addition, efforts to provide a closer link between income support and access to serious job training and job placement need to be encouraged. Recent reforms require all states to conduct job training programs for persons receiving welfare, but such programs are often minimal, providing little training or education and encouraging placement in jobs that offer minimum wages and no health insurance, thus leaving many families worse off than before.

This litany of proposals could continue–for education, for housing, for economic development, and for all the other issues related to poverty and need in this country. The point is that there are workable and possible programs available in the policy arena. The problem is the lack of political will to implement and fund such programs.

Other Policy Issues Relating to Economic Justice Concerns

Although I have discussed domestic poverty issues extensively as an example, there are a wide variety of other policy areas in which similar analysis could occur. Here is a sampling of these areas:

1. **Environmental stewardship.** A wide variety of policy proposals are under discussion, designed to limit further environmental destruction or to assist in cleaning up past environmental damage. These include international treaties on air pollution control, increased national funding for hazardous waste cleanup, and stronger efforts to encourage local recycling.

2. **Shifting priorities away from war and toward peace.** There are many proposals to reorient the national and the world economies away from massive amounts of military spending and toward programs that invest in jobs, education, and people. On the international front, many groups are working to extend treaties designed to reduce nuclear

armaments and to limit arms sales. Nationally, the collapse of Communism in eastern Europe provides an opportunity to reduce troop and other military commitments in the federal budget over the long term. At a local level, communities need to develop alternate job opportunities for workers who would lose their jobs in a conversion away from military production.

3. The international debt crisis and developing countries. The explosion of debt among developing countries in the 1970s has left many poor countries with financial commitments that drain their treasuries. A substantial amount of their national income goes to repay debt rather than to invest in an improved economy for their citizens. The U.S. treasury is engaged in ongoing international negotiations designed to address these problems. Debt forgiveness and debt reduction, particularly for the poorest nations, will be necessary. In addition, the very low levels of development aid provided by the United States, as compared with other countries, also limits our involvement in the developing world. Increases in U.S. development aid have been proposed by many church-related groups, along with a redirection of U.S. military assistance into more broadly based aid categories.

This list could go on for many more pages. The underlying goal of this discussion is to look for policies that promote greater economic opportunities for a broader group of persons, and to seek actively those policies that promise a positive answer to the question "What does this do for the poor?"

Stepping Forward in Faith

There is no final answer to the question "But are we sure this is the right thing to do?" There are many examples of well-intentioned efforts at reform that backfire, but there are also many examples of such efforts that succeed. Our knowledge and our ability to forecast the future are limited. At best, we can learn from our failures. No one, including persons in the church, can offer guarantees that a particular policy proposal will succeed. However, doing nothing because we do not know the best thing to do—particularly in the policy arena—is not an option. If we enact no antipoverty programs, people will go hungry and homeless. Our current set of proposed changes may not (almost surely will not) eliminate poverty, but if the evidence indicates that these programs will make things better on the margin—that some groups will be better off than they are now–then we are justified in publicly supporting such changes. As in so many other areas of our life, good public policy requires at times that we step forward in faith. The economic pain of too many of our brothers and sisters is too great for us to remain inactive.

Summary

There is no direct way to move from biblical lessons to policy proposals. As a result, individuals and churches must exercise discernment in their analysis of policy issues. Although our religious faith provides general principles for thinking about public issues, specific policy proposals must emerge from the prayer, wisdom, and experience of those who struggle to interpret the meaning of an active faith in today's world. This requires study as well as good intentions. The difficulty of the task, however, should not immobilize our efforts. The church and individuals can address public policy issues by speaking out against present injustices, providing alternative frameworks for analysis, and proposing specific policy changes. The questions "What does this do for the poor?" and "How can we increase the inclusiveness and equity of our economic system?" can lead to an effective agenda for reform.

GROUP DISCUSSION AND ACTIVITIES
Suggested Group Exercise

Select a topic of concern to your local community that people are likely to know something about (jobs, public school quality, or adequate police protection, for instance).

Divide participants into small groups of about five persons each. Ask each group to discuss (1) What is the nature of the problem? (2) What types of public policy might address this problem? (3) What groups should be involved in talking about and deciding on any policy changes (voters, parents, city council, workers, the state government, or others)? (4) How can our local church be involved in working on this issue?

The main point of this exercise is to get people involved in a discussion of a particular problem and to think about how interested groups can work toward a public policy change. You may want to tailor the questions to the particular issue you select.

When the small groups have completed their discussion, come together in the large group and compare the policies discussed in the various small groups.

Starting Discussion Questions

1. This chapter proposes that the concept of "economic rights" become part of the American approach to poverty. Do persons in the United States have a right to adequate food, shelter, health care, and education? How would these rights differ from or be similar to political rights? Would you support a constitutional amendment that contained a statement of economic rights?

2. The discussion in this chapter recognizes that not all proposed public policy changes are effective. List some legislative changes that you think have improved the lives of the poor in this country. Indicate some legislative changes, meant to help the poor, that you think might not have helped. What is the difference between them?

3. Ask someone in the congregation or community who works on public policy issues to talk briefly about how policy decisions are made. Who decides what is "good" policy? What determines which laws get passed and which fail? In what role can the church and church members be involved?

CHAPTER 10

Facing the Hard Issues: No One Said Change Would Be Easy

Our lives are deeply interconnected with the lives of persons all over the world. Jesus, answering the question "Who is my neighbor?" makes it clear that there are no boundaries that define neighbors inside and strangers outside. Few aspects of our modern lives reflect this human interconnectedness more than the economic ties that reach around the world, binding our daily economic decisions with the life and work of persons in Los Angeles, Tokyo, San Salvador, Cairo–everywhere.

God calls us to an active concern for the welfare of all our neighbors, both near and far. Through prophets both ancient and modern, we are reminded that God's people are to do justice. When the hungry are fed, when the oppressed are freed from prison, when all are included in the household and economy of God, then we do honor to God. This chapter discusses some of the barriers to action and understanding that often limit our commitment to economic justice.

How Much Am I Willing to Change My Life?

God calls us to transform our lives, to recognize the needs and desires of our neighbors and to work on lessening human need and economic injustice. This is a difficult call to hear. Our own desire for personal economic security is strong. Hearing that hundreds of millions are poor around the globe is deeply threatening for persons who are not poor. If we are called to give to all in need, we may be left with nothing ourselves. Few of us are any braver than the young man who, upon hearing that he must give up all his possessions to follow Jesus, turns sadly away. If faithfulness to God requires utter selflessness to our own needs and desires, then few of us will answer the call to be faithful Christians. Although we admire and honor the outstanding individuals whose lives seem completely selfless–Francis of Assisi, Gandhi, Dorothy Day, Mother Teresa–few of us are so moved by their example that we join them.

I recall a church discussion group in which we were talking about the question "How much should I give?" One woman was silent through much of the discussion, but toward the end she leaned forward and said something like this: "Some days I feel terribly guilty that I live in suburban America while people starve elsewhere. I don't know how to deal with that very well. I think the best answer that I've found is a combination of prayer and action. Whenever we have silent prayers in church, I confess how little I do compared with how much I have. I've tried to change my life, at least in little ways, and I try to give a little more of my time and money each year. I keep asking myself, 'Can I do more?' But I also have to recognize my limits. The best I can do for God is to keep asking myself uncomfortable questions and to keep trying."

This woman has found a way to integrate her concerns for justice and for the well-being of her neighbors into her own life. Her actions might not make a large difference in the world, but they can make a difference in the lives of the people affected by the money she gives or the projects she works on.

The Importance of Listening

A fundamental prerequisite to understanding the needs and problems of our neighbors is to listen to them, talk with them, and learn more about their lives. All of us come from a specific economic history; we each have an economic story that shapes our lives and the lives of our parents and grandparents. It is always tempting to assume that others have been shaped in the same way and that their stories and their economic histories lead them to a similar view of the world.

Justice is often in the eye of the beholder. Some persons see injustice in situations where others see only inevitable reality. Those who spoke for the abolition of slavery in the nineteenth century in this country confronted those who saw slavery as part of the "natural order" created by God. Those who are not in slavery, who are not unjustly imprisoned, who are not hungry, or who are not homeless, often have difficulty understanding the stories of those who have experienced these conditions.

Thus, *listening* is a fundamental exercise for those who would speak for and seek justice. Too often in past history, persons in the church have tried to improve the lives of the poor–typically with the best of intentions–without trying to understand the world that the poor themselves experience. The most effective way to assist people is not to do something to them or for them, but to empower them to bring about change in their own lives. This requires understanding their lives, working with them rather than working for them.

Listening can occur in many ways. Through the church, we have access to the stories and concerns of persons around the world. Through the world media, we can visit people's homes and listen to them talk. In our own community, we can attend events and become involved in groups that give us a chance to talk with and work with others whose backgrounds are very different from our own. Through such efforts, other people become not just "them" or "the poor" or "foreigners," but acquire faces and names and lives that connect to our own lives.

Moving from Faith to Action

On Sunday morning we are all people of faith. We worship, we confess, and we pray. We are renewed spiritually. On Monday morning it is often less clear how this faith interacts with our lives. In particular, it is often difficult to discern how to move from faith–from a spiritual commitment–to informed action.

Particularly for Americans from a mainstream Protestant background, such movement is difficult because we are often taught to be wary of excessive emotion. Worship is done "in good order," sermons are intellectual presentations, and adult education involves a friendly and dispassionate discussion of selected issues. How, then, do we allow ourselves to be gripped by faith commitments so strong that they lead us to transform our lives? How do we allow ourselves to let the spiritual and emotional energy of faith shape our well-ordered lives?

This is a particularly difficult problem when the changes being discussed involve our economic lives. Economics and faith have been separated for so long that it seems awkward even to begin thinking about them together. To find the energy that will help us draw connections between Sunday and Monday morning, we need to do several things.

First, we need to recognize the simplicity of God's demand for justice. All human beings are brothers and sisters to us. Their well-being is our concern. As agents in God's household, we are to see that all are included and have the resources necessary for life. These are not complex concepts. Their motivating power lies precisely in their simplicity. Jesus' command, "You shall love your neighbor as yourself [Matt. 22:39]" has transformed people's lives for centuries because of the power in its straightforward simplicity. The linkage between faith and economics is, at its core, a commitment to a few very simple and straightforward faith precepts. The simplicity of these core ideas enables us to believe them and understand them at the gut level where faith is formed. We do not need a complex theology to understand Micah's words, "And what does the Lord require of you but to do justice, and to love kindness, and to walk humbly with your God? [Mic. 6:8]"

Second, the application of faith to our lives requires prayerful consideration. What changes do we make in our own lives? What issues do we commit ourselves to working on? Whose need do we respond to? There are no simple and uniform rules; each person must find his or her own route from faith to action.

One of the most difficult problems facing any person seeking personal or social change is to avoid despair and burnout. Despite all the energy that any person can bring to an effort, change comes slowly. I remember a person named Rhonda who showed up at several meetings of a local antinuclear citizen action group in which I was involved. Rhonda had seen a recent TV show on the dangers of nuclear weapons and decided to commit herself to working for their abolition. She attended three meetings, full of energy, full of prophecy, full of commitment. She then disappeared. Several months later, at a meeting I was attending to work on hunger issues in the state, Rhonda showed up again. She had just seen a documentary on Ethiopia and decided to become involved in fighting hunger. Again, she came to a few meetings and then lost interest.

Rhonda is like most of us. She has wonderful intentions, she really means well, but she finds it hard to keep creating time and energy to work on issues such as economic justice and peace when such efforts typically don't show many short-term rewards. There are several ways to avoid Rhonda's problem:

1. Do some things that promise an immediate reward. Most people aren't very good at working only on global change, because they never see any results of their work. Although we need people to write letters, lobby congresspersons, and try to change national laws, this work can be combined with other more immediately rewarding work. Working at the local recycling center shows you how many tons of paper are being recycled in your community. Serving at the local soup kitchen lets you say, "these fifty people had a good meal tonight, in part because I was there." Do some things that let you *see* the tangible effects of your efforts.

2. Find a support community. Whether through your church or through a group of friends with similar concerns, find people to talk to, to work with, and to share frustrations with. I recall how deeply discouraged many of us were in the early 1980s when major federal legislation was passed limiting a wide range of child nutrition and antipoverty programs. I went to a meeting of my church's social action committee where all we did was complain. We mourned together for our failures and felt very overwhelmed and hopeless. After a while, prodding each other, we went back to work to try to reverse some of the changes. It would have been much harder alone.

3. Recognize your limits; avoid burnout. It is often far better to keep working on things steadily and consistently than to exert a great spurt of energy and then be overwhelmed by exhaustion. There's no reason to feel guilty because your family and job commitments limit how much you can do elsewhere. Committing yourself to do something doesn't mean you've committed yourself to do everything. We all need vacations at times, not just from our paid jobs, but from other commitments as well. Healthy churches and organizations rotate leadership and rotate commitments. It's wise to take time to renew and refresh our own souls.

But I Don't Know Enough

Probably the most common barrier to getting involved in issues—particularly issues of economic justice and human need—is a sense that "I'm just not ready. I don't know enough. I'll leave this to the experts." Some part of this feeling is fear of the unknown. I recall the fear and uncertainty I felt when I first volunteered to stay overnight at a homeless shelter. Who would these people be? What would happen during the evening? How should I act? When we get involved in things we don't know much about, we often fear we'll make fools of ourselves.

I work at a university, which is a place where everyone always wants to know more. The more deeply I become involved in a research project, the more I realize how much I don't know and how vast the subject is. This realization can enrich my work by opening up new research questions and new ways of looking at my data. I have seen researchers, however, who are paralyzed by this realization. Their research is never finished, the book is never written, because there are always unanswered questions.

Few of us are experts on anything. In fact, knowledge is often created by experience and involvement. As we become involved in an issue, we learn more about it. As we learn more about it, our understanding and our involvement changes. Action and knowledge are simultaneous. If we refuse to get involved in a group working on the lack of low income housing in our community because we don't know enough about mortgages and construction and house financing, then we will never learn more.

Of course, if wisdom is acquired only slowly (sometimes it seems that wisdom is never acquired at all), this means we all do things that later look like mistakes. We might write a letter about an urgent concern and later decide that it was a bad idea. We might give money to an organization whose director turns out to be untrustworthy. Our church might support a peace organization that collapses in six months because it wasn't well organized. Even extensive knowledge and preparation can't prevent mistakes, but engaging in social change is a risky business and making mistakes is how we learn. Anyone who is unwilling to make a mistake is also unwilling to make a commitment that might turn out well.

Faith is a necessary element in work for economic justice and economic change. Our first involvement in an issue—as individuals or as a church—must be done with faith and hope, without fully knowing where it will lead us. As we learn a bit more, we may draw back and look for a different issue, or we may be drawn into a deeper involvement, leading to further commitment.

Commitment arises from and is nourished by action, and action is necessary to sustain commitment. Similarly, knowledge and understanding grow with action and commitment. The "experts" are those who get involved and learn from their experiences.

Who Will Lose?

Ultimately, a commitment to economic justice confronts an extremely difficult dilemma: if we are to make the world a more equitable and more just place, some of us will have less than we do now. Perhaps in the very long run all persons can have access to the resources now used by middle-class Americans. But such a dream is currently far from reality. Few of those who now live in material security find that a comforting statement.

There is no promise in the Bible that all will be better off in a more just world. In fact, in biblical situations when justice is administered, those in power lose their riches. Repentance spares their lives, but not their wealth. The moral of these stories is clear: those who store riches for themselves on earth will find neither security nor God's favor.

There is a strong temptation in any discussion of economic justice to envision a utopian possibility in which all are better off. In such a vision the once-poor receive the abundance that lets them leave poverty behind; the once-rich lose some of their wealth but are more than compensated by a new sense of community and spiritual enrichment. The implication is that if we can just get the message out to most people–if we can simply convert enough people to true Christianity–economic justice will flower as more and more individuals transform their lives. There is little historical evidence that such conversions are likely to occur for large numbers of people or to change an entire society.

A Question of Power

No Christian can ignore the power of individual conversion. Yet a commitment to global economic justice is naive when it relies on all persons in a complex and diverse society "seeing the light" and substantively transforming their own lives and the institutions around them. Thus, the question of power arises. How do we, as Christians, confront and challenge power when we believe it is being misused? What power do we claim and use for ourselves? How do we avoid the corrupting influence of power in those who wield it?

These issues demand an entire book themselves, but let me make a few brief comments about how to approach them. First, it is precisely because working on social change requires confronting power that justice and peace issues must be linked by the church. Procedures for nonviolent resistance and peaceful conflict resolution are techniques that the church must develop as ways to confront and use power without resorting to violence and hostility.

The self-declaration of the United Church of Christ that it is a Just Peace Church is an effort toward dealing with these issues. Ideally, it says that the church will not tolerate injustices, but, in confronting the structures of injustice, will seek avenues of change that avoid aggression and human destruction. When faced with injustice, the church and its members may rightfully respond with anger, but because of its commitment to peace, the church will seek effective, nonhostile ways to express that anger. This is not an easy task; perhaps in some situations it is impossible. The church, however, is the primary institution whose mission commits it to seeking and modeling the possibility that power can be confronted and overcome without violence or aggression.

Second, the struggle of individuals and the church for social change necessarily means becoming involved in the power games that occur everywhere in this world. There is no way to maintain a "purity" above the struggle. Some persons have argued that the church must keep itself apart from the powers and principalities of this world. But doing and being are inseparable in the Christian faith. The church is *both* of this world and not of this world. "Feed the hungry and care for the sick" is one of Jesus' strongest and most frequently repeated lessons. When this means violating the laws that say no healing can occur on the Sabbath, Jesus makes it clear that human need is more important than laws.

The church and its members have a mission in this world that will necessarily lead to ongoing dialogue, confrontation, and potential conflict with governments, laws, and secular powers. This is not an optional and foolish choice, but an inevitable result of the faith to which we are called. Nor is it an excuse for the church to gather and exercise secular power. Only when the church works to remain an open institution, not controlled by any one ethnic group, political party, or political perspective, can the church speak authoritatively out of its moral convictions.

The Ambiguity of Being an American: Powerful and Powerless

One of the deepest ambiguities faced by most American Christians is their individual sense of powerlessness, even as they recognize their powerful role as a nation. On the one hand, few Americans feel personally powerful. Most families struggle with budgets, jobs, and each other's demands for love and recognition. When asked to describe themselves economically, most Americans call themselves middle class–neither rich nor poor. Many of us feel as though we have little control over anything beyond a limited range of issues in our own lives. We are victims of recession and inflation. We are subject to the demands of our work. We do what has to be done, when it has to be done, because there are no other alternatives.

Yet, we also recognize that America is a powerful nation. Even the poor among us are among the rich of the world. Although we rarely think of it, we know–even as we struggle with our own personal budgets–that we have more economic choices and possibilities than our ancestors could have dreamed of.

Thinking about the link between our faith and our economic lives requires resolving some of these ambiguities. It requires recognizing our limits: Most of us are involved in a web of economic responsibilities toward spouses, parents, and children that we take seriously and that realistically do limit our ability to change and to act. But resolving the dilemma also requires recognizing our potential. Even in the midst of these limits, there are many things we can do. We are citizens of a country that supports and encourages citizen action. Most of us have real control over many aspects of our lifestyles. Most of us can afford to give–some time, some energy, some money.

If we feel victimized, we lose any sense of possibility for change. If we dwell on our political and economic riches as Americans, we can be overwhelmed by our responsibilities in a hungry world. Ultimately, we need to recognize our personal limits, without feeling guilty or inadequate because of them, at the same time that we also recognize our potential for commitment and change.

Summary

Working toward change–whether personal or social–is always difficult. We must struggle to understand what it is that God demands of us. We have to recognize our limits, to do those things which we can do and not become discouraged by the dozens of things which we cannot do. We will be helped in deciding what we can do by listening to others and learning their stories. Even as we struggle to understand what our faith commitments mean, we can be motivated by the fundamental simplicity of the call to love our neighbor and to do justice. To carry this out, however, requires that we find others who share our concerns and that we avoid overcommitment and burnout. We must not be immobilized by a sense of inadequacy or lack of knowledge. Action, commitment, and knowledge all grow simultaneously. Finally, it is important to realize that there are very hard questions involved in issues of global economic justice that Americans find particularly difficult to face. Not all will be better off in a world with greater economic inclusiveness. Working for economic justice means confronting our own fear of economic insecurity. It means dealing with the question of power and working on solutions that confront and challenge power without resorting to violence.

GROUP DISCUSSION AND ACTIVITIES

Suggested Group Exercise

Give each person a piece of paper. By themselves, have them write down three things they could do that could be a step toward transforming their lives to be more aware of economic justice issues. These need not be big actions; for instance, a list might include such things as "increase my giving to church missions," "read the newspaper daily," "pray regularly," "write a letter to my representative on budget cuts." Then have each person list the barriers to action in her or his own life–the other activities that interfere, the fears, the hesitations, and so on. After everyone has thought about this alone, ask each person to get together with one other person, share the lists, and talk about how these barriers could be overcome.

Starting Discussion Questions

1. This chapter argues that action and commitment are simultaneous. Can you give examples in your own life of how getting involved in something (perhaps accidentally) led to a new set of commitments? If action and commitment occur together, what implications does this have for our religious life? For instance, what does it imply about the value of regular worship attendance?

2. Do you agree with the statement that part of the power of Jesus' command to love your neighbor as yourself lies in its simplicity? Why is simplicity important? What other religious or political statements might be equally powerful because of their simplicity?

3. Many people become very uncomfortable when "power" and "the church" are discussed together. This chapter argues that the church will necessarily have to engage in power struggles and confront laws and governments in speaking a message of economic justice. How do you respond? How might the church engage in such activity in a faithful and "churchly" way?

4. What is your response when you hear of people, such as Mother Teresa, who have truly transformed their lives to help the poor?

Do Justice

The Gospel of Luke records that the start of Jesus' ministry began in Nazareth where he went to the synagogue, stood up, and began to read from a scroll. He selected a passage from Isaiah and read, "The Spirit of the Lord is upon me, because the Lord has anointed me to bring good news to the poor. God has sent me to proclaim release to the captives and recovery of sight to the blind, to let the oppressed go free, to proclaim the year of the Lord's favor [Luke 4:18–19]."

To the amazement of his audience, all well-known and life-long neighbors and friends, Jesus then announces that this scripture is now to be fulfilled and goes on to give examples of how God's favor comes even to two enemies of Israel. How do his friends respond? Luke records that "when they heard this, all in the synagogue were filled with rage. They got up, drove him out of the town, and led him to the brow of the hill on which their town was built, so that they might hurl him off the cliff [Luke 4: 28–29]."

Two thousand years have passed. What would we hear if Jesus were to return, stand up in our church one Sunday morning, and proclaim his ministry anew? He might say something like this:

The Spirit of the Lord is upon me. God's presence flows through my life and through yours as well. The Spirit who made my ministry possible 2000 years ago still moves through the world today, changing history and transforming lives.

Because the Lord has anointed me to bring good news to the poor. I am astonished by the wealth of America; surely no one can be hungry or thirsty in a land this rich. I do not understand your talk of poverty and homelessness. Did you not hear my words? Must you still ask, "Who is my neighbor?" For those who build my church there must never be a division between East and West or North and South. If

147

I were hungry, would you give me food? If I were thirsty, would you give me water? Then why do you refuse to help the poor persons and nations who cry out around you?

God has sent me to proclaim release to the captives and recovery of sight to the blind. I seek a world where the ill and uninsured shall receive medical care and the illiterate shall have schools for their children; where homes that were condemned shall be rebuilt and the land that was taken from the poor shall be returned; where the polluted air shall blow clear and the hazardous waste dumps shall be made clean; where the unemployed shall find fruitful work and those who profit from the trade in arms and military hardware shall convert their factories to peacetime production.

To let the oppressed go free. I seek a world where political prisoners shall be released and people shall demand a voice in the governments that rule them; where the wealthy nations shall forgive the debts of the poor and large corporations will be committed to the communities where their workers live and work.

To proclaim the year of the Lord's favor. You whom I see around me have been given many gifts. I call on you and on your church to demonstrate your commitment to my teachings. Give of your money; give of your time; be active citizens; let the Spirit transform your lives and transform the life of your church so that it reflects your faithfulness to the Lord. The Lord will find favor with those who are faithful.

How would your church respond to Jesus' words?

First Story Ending

When they heard this, all in the congregation were enraged. They got up, drove him to the airport, and told him never to return.

Second Story Ending

When they heard this, all in the congregation were filled with the Spirit of the Lord. Together, they knelt and confessed their sin. And after their prayers were over, they sat down together, and some promised to speak with their families about their church giving, and some promised to work on affordable housing in the community, and some promised to travel to Central American and bring back a report on the concerns of the poor in those countries, and some promised to go over the church budget to see how they could arrange to pay for health insurance for their secretary. And when they had discussed all these things, they went out into the community and did as they had promised.

Which ending would occur in your congregation?

United Church of Christ Pronouncement on Christian Faith: Economic Life and Justice

This is the text of the Pronouncement passed by General Synod 17 of the United Church of Christ in July 1989.

I. Summary

This pronouncement is an affirmation by the United Church of Christ that the struggle to achieve economic justice for all of God's people is an imperative of the Christian faith. It is also a confession that we have done too little to correct the economic injustices of our nation and the world. Finally, it is a statement of our commitment to transform the structures of church and society by working for economic justice.

II. Background

There is a sickness in the soul that infects both the poor and the affluent in our nation and the world as a result of economic injustice. Among the poor are those who have internalized economic powerlessness and poverty, losing a sense of meaning and worth to their lives. Among the affluent are those who have been captured by the false values and priorities of materialism and who have also lost a sense of the meaning and purpose of life. An unjust economy generates dissatisfaction for both those with too much and those with too little.

For Christians, economic justice is a faith issue, "for the Lord is a God of justice [Isa. 30:18]." Scripture discloses a God whose love and compassion for creation have no limits, a God "who executes justice for the oppressed; who gives food to the hungry [Ps. 146:7]," a God who in Jesus Christ came "that they may have life, and have it abundantly" (John 10:10). Moreover, there is pervasive poverty and suffering in the midst of those economic systems which are capable of organizing the gifts of creation so that all members of the human household could have the means of life. In such a situation, commitment to economic justice becomes a profound human responsibility. In the parable of the great judgment, Jesus reminds individuals and nations that in failing to provide food to the hungry, drink to the thirsty, welcome to the stranger, clothing to the naked, and care to the infirmed and imprisoned "as you did it not to one of the least of these, you did it not to me [Matt. 25:45]."

This pronouncement attempts to portray the experiences and perspectives of both those victimized by present economic systems as well as those who benefit from those systems. It is motivated by the cries of anguish of our sisters and brothers in our nation and the world. Remembering God's special concern for the poor and suffering, the pronouncement seeks to understand why current economic systems fail to provide an adequate means of life for two thirds of the members of the human community.

The *Pronouncement on Christian Faith: Economic Life and Justice* builds on the *Pronouncement Affirming the United Church of Christ as a Just Peace Church* voted by the Fifteenth General Synod. It presents the call to economic justice as a complement to the focus on peace in that earlier *Pronouncement*.

The *Pronouncement* is the outgrowth of a long process of study and reflection. In 1980, a group of United Church of Christ theologians and economists made a covenant together "to join the search for new economic theories and strategies more faithful to the Gospel." The Fourteenth General Synod requested the preparation of a pronouncement containing an analysis of the global economic crisis from a Christian perspective, an articulation of a public theology of economics, and an appropriate response by the United Church of Christ.

This *Pronouncement* is the synthesis of two documents: the *Proposed Pronouncement on Christian Faith and Economic Life* and the *Proposed Pronouncement on Christian Faith and Economic Justice*, both of which have been submitted to the Seventeenth General Synod. The proposed *Pronouncement on Christian Faith and Economic Life* was informed by feedback to the study paper, *Christian Faith and Economic Life*, provided by a diverse group of United Church of Christ members. The racial and ethnic members of the United Church of Christ believed that the relationship between racism and economic injustice needed further articulation; this was provided in the *Proposed Pronouncement on Christian Faith and Economic Justice.*

This *Pronouncement* recognizes that the majority of people in the world suffer in one way or another under the present global economic order, irrespective of their particular economic systems. As North American Christians in the United Church of Christ, we must boldly confess the inequity and injustice in the economic system of the United States, at the same time that we admit our involvement with injustices in the global economy. This confession requires both naming the structural problems inherent in our economic system and confronting the effects of racism, sexism, materialism, and militarism. The church cannot be truly prophetic without honest confession.

As we struggle to understand the demands of justice that God places on our economic lives, we acknowledge that we, in the United Church of Christ, come from many different economic backgrounds. Our personal histories affect how we hear the Word, particularly when economic issues are at stake. Thus, rich and poor in our church respond very differently to the news that the hungry were fed and the rich sent away empty (Luke 1:53). Some who are poor among us hear this Word and cry out for immediate change. Some who are affluent among us let the fear of loss keep us from fully hearing the judging and transforming message. Those who are comfortable often focus on the benefits of the current economic system and hope that charity and economic growth will ameliorate suffering and poverty. But those whose children go to bed hungry at night, those who have no home or means of income, cannot wait.

This *Pronouncement* is being offered by the United Church Board for World Ministries, the United Church Board for Homeland Ministries, the Commission for Racial Justice, the Office for Church in Society, and the Council for Racial and Ethnic Ministries.

III. Biblical, Ethical and Theological Rationale

The word "economy" comes from two Greek words meaning "household", and "law" or "management". (The compounded Greek word is often translated "stewardship.") Economy therefore is the ordering or management of the household. For Christians, economics involves the management of the human household in a manner consistent with God's intentions as revealed in scripture. Many of the biblical traditions depict God's desire for a just household in which all persons, particularly the poor and vulnerable, have access to resources sufficient for survival, freedom, dignity, and community participation.

The formative event of biblical faith is the Exodus, God's liberation of slaves from the oppressive household or economy of Pharaoh. God disrupts the productive but deadly economy of Pharaoh because some of its slaves cry out to God under their burdens. After delivering the people of Israel, God establishes a covenanted household of justice in the land of promise. The first five books of the Old Testament describe a three-way covenant linking God, the human family, and the whole earth, balancing the needs of humanity and of nature (Leviticus 25:1–7, 11–12). The covenant makes clear that economic activity should be ordered to reflect the mutual obligations between God and the human community. Israel's economy should be grounded in God's justice.

Repeatedly, the covenant of the Old Testament focuses on the needs and rights of those who often are excluded from the community. The rules of God's household demand that the poor (Exodus 23:6, Deuteronomy 15:7–11), the stranger (Exodus 22:21–24), the sojourner (Deuteronomy 10:19), and the widow and orphan (Exodus 22:22) all be accorded special protection and access to the livelihood of the household for the sake of God's grace to Israel ("for you were strangers in the land of Egypt" [Exod. 22:21]"). The Sabbath and Jubilee Years urge a just ordering for overcoming exploitation through property redistribution and care of the earth. God's household is ordered to protect its weakest and most vulnerable members

(Leviticus 25:8-22). The same God who brings the universe into being and provides the earth with abundance intends that the needs of all God's creatures be met (Genesis 1:27–31). God's justice (Psalm 99:4) is opposed to patterns of economic inequality and power that leave some marginalized and others dispossessed.

When Israel establishes an empire with a king, the poor, the weak, and the oppressed become central to God's economic concern. In the household of Israel, the king was called to have concern for the weak, save the lives of the poor, and liberate them from oppression and violence (Psalm 72:12-14, cf. Jeremiah 22:15-16). When their ordering of Israel's household generates affluence but exploits or ignores the poor, God's prophets challenge Israel's kings to account. Prophetic denunciation of such royal economic policy is pervasive in the Old Testament, and prophetic judgment includes the warning that God will disrupt the order of Israel's household for the sake of the poor even as God has disrupted Pharaoh's household (Isaiah 10:1-3, Amos 4:1-2, Jeremiah 22:13-14).

In Jesus, God becomes poor (2 Corinthians 8:9) and shares the suffering, the life, and the death of the poor and dispossessed. God in Jesus Christ reigns as no other ruler, not set above, but in suffering love with all people. It is this God who is God in every dimension of our life–spiritual and economic, secular and sacred (Psalm 24:1; Colossians 1:15-21). According to the Gospel of Luke, Jesus inaugurates his public ministry by announcing that he has been anointed to preach good news to the poor, to proclaim liberty to the captives, and to set at liberty the oppressed (Luke 4:18). Jesus' public ministry is the announcement that God's household is open to all to whom it had been systematically closed by rules of the world's economy.

The world of Jesus is the world of Rome, a most efficient, successful, and yet corrupt political economy. The empire's economy, for those who were able and willing to compete successfully within its household rules, was at its peak. Yet the focus of Jesus' life and ministry was not these people. In his preaching we encounter again and again a challenge to economic greed and oppression which are based on the values of accumulation and exploitation. In the sayings and actions of Jesus the reign of God's justice reverses precisely those values upon which the human economy depends for its success:

Blessed are you poor . . .
    Woe to you who are rich . . .
Blessed are you who hunger . . .
    Woe to you who are full . . .
Blessed are you who weep . . .
    Woe to you who laugh . . .
Blessed are you when people despise you and exclude you . . .
    Woe to you when people speak well of you . . .
                                        —Luke 6:20–26

Through his own table fellowship among the excluded, his signs and wonders among the outcasts, and in his crucifixion outside the gates, Jesus took on himself the suffering of God with the poor and all who are excluded from justice within the household. Through Jesus' resurrection God proclaims that abundant life is for all. In Christ, the covenant of love and justice in the household is made new and is expanded to the whole human family. The early church, in faithfulness to Jesus' life, death, and resurrection, held in tension the coming reign of God and the values which undergird the human economy. In ordering its household the early church rejected many of the principles operative within the larger economy. In its expectation of God's reign, it embraced both the life of the community as the basic motivation for economic production and human need as the basic principle of distribution within the household of God (Acts 2:44–45). It sought to follow Jesus' own orientation to those marginalized by the injustice of the political economy (James 5:4–6).

The reign of God coming in our midst is a continual invitation to repentance, for all economic systems fall short of reflecting the household of God and the covenant is continually breached by injustice. As Christians we must acknowledge that we cannot witness to the reign of God and also serve mammon (Mt. 6:24). Our economic lives are as subject to God's grace and God's judgment as our spiritual lives. We shrink from this acknowledgment, however, because we are afraid to bear the suffering love of Christ in our own lives. We resist because we find our own vested interests challenged if we are faithful to God's covenant. We hesitate, for to acknowledge the reign of God and justice is to expose our loyalty to mammon and we are unmasked as idolaters. Yet it is promised that through faith, hope, and love God can bring our lives into repentance. We are both haunted and energized by the certainty that God will continue to judge us, transform us, and empower us until the rule of justice prevails in the human household.

Through our baptism into the body of Christ we are commissioned to participate with God in the just reordering of our economy. We stand under the demand of God that the economy be reorganized so that the poor may also share in the abundance of creation and be poor no more (Deuteronomy 15:4-5). As stewards of the household, we are called to care for creation so that all members of the household will have "their portion of food at the proper time [Luke 12:42]."

IV. Suffering Within the Household of God

A. Poverty and Affluence

I am a citizen of the United States and a child of God, and so are my children. We are not just statistics. We are real human beings.
(Cheryl Kramer, mother of four from Iowa)

Cheryl Kramer was forced by her economic situation to give up her children to foster care. Theirs is the human anguish behind the statistic that families with children are the "fastest growing" segment of the homeless, according to a recent National Academy of Sciences study. There are over 100,000 children homeless each night, and perhaps a quarter million children who experienced homelessness at some time during 1988.

Within the United States, one of the wealthiest countries in the world, economic growth and affluence have not eliminated significant levels of poverty. In 1987, 8.2 percent of white families lived below the poverty level. With respect to white families and African American families with a female head of household, 26.7 percent and 51.8 percent respectively lived below the poverty level. One fifth of all children in this country live in poor households. Moreover, the burden of poverty falls disproportionately on a few groups—African Americans, Hispanic Americans, Native Americans, Pacific Islanders and Asian Americans, women who head households, children, and persons with disabilities. African American and Hispanic American families are nearly three times more likely to be poor than white families, and the incidence of poverty is even higher among Native Americans. Growing numbers of homeless persons inhabit our streets. Because of poverty, millions of Americans are without adequate nutrition, health care, and shelter.

On a global level, the overwhelming majority of the human family confront poverty, poor health, and lack of education. One in five lives in absolute and dehumanizing poverty, facing a daily struggle to survive. Although the world food supply can provide enough for all, some 770 million people do not get sufficient food for an active and healthy life. Persistent hunger throughout the world dooms new generations of children to prolonged problems caused by severe malnutrition at an early age. There are more adult illiterates, more unemployed, more persons suffering from ill health, and more people unable to satisfy their basic needs for food and clean water than there were 25 years ago.

The gap between degrading poverty and dazzling wealth has become evermore pronounced. In the United States, the wealthiest 20 percent of all households own 75 percent of all assets and earn almost half of all income, and these shares have increased during the past decade. At a global level, the disparities in income are enormous and increasing. In 1983, 20 percent of the world's population received 68 percent of the world's income. Low income countries in Asia, Africa, and Central America, with nearly half the world's population, account for only 5 percent of global income. During the past ten years, standards of living in the poorest countries have fallen further behind.

B. Racism

The historical record of how white Europeans conquered North America by destroying the native population and how they then built their new nation's economy on the backs of kidnapped Africans who had been turned into chattel are facts that can hardly be denied. . . .White America has yet to recognize the extent of its racism—that we are and have always been a racist society—much less to repent of its racial sins. (Jim Wallis, editor of *Sojourners Magazine*)

Racism is the systematized oppression of one race by another. In 1984, the National Council of Churches defined racism as "racial prejudice plus power." This position maintains that privileges conferred upon the majority by virtue of its racial origins are supported by a self-sustaining system of institutions and structures which economically benefits from racism. Hence, the Commission for Racial Justice of the United Church of Christ defined racism as "economically-empowered racial prejudice and discrimination."

In specific terms, these policies translate into an unemployment rate in American Indian communities ranging from 70 to 90 percent. Alcoholism, and other forms of substance abuse, has touched about 90 percent of individuals in the American Indian community. Hispanic Americans, 85 percent of whom live in urban areas, are a disproportionately poor group living in substandard inner-city housing. The poverty rate for Hispanics was 28.2 percent in 1987, significantly higher than the already elevated rate of 21.9 percent in 1977. Over the last eight to ten years, poverty spread more rapidly among Hispanics than among any other group. Likewise, economic motivations played a role in the internment of Japanese Americans during World War II, when war hysteria was used as a smoke screen for the stealing of land and other possessions. The majority of Japanese Americans in Hawaii were not put in concentration camps because most of them were lowly paid pineapple and sugar plantation workers in 1942. Japanese Americans, however, owned land in California and were supplying approximately 90 percent of the vegetable crop in the state.

African Americans, who were forcibly brought to the United States as slaves, continue to suffer from economic exploitation. Their unemployment rate in 1986 was 14.5 percent as compared with a white unemployment rate of 6.0 percent. African Americans between ages 16 and 19 suffered a staggering unemployment rate of 39.3 percent. Today, whites enjoy 12 times the net worth of African Americans. The median net worth of African American households is $3,400, compared to $39,100 for white households. Unfortunately, Martin Luther King's words still apply: "There were slaves when [the Declaration of Independence] was written; there were slaves when it was adopted; and to this day, black Americans do not have life, liberty nor the privilege of pursuing happiness, and millions of poor white Americans are in economic bondage that is scarcely less oppressive."

C. Militarization

In the councils of Government, we must guard against the acquisition of unwarranted influence, whether sought or unsought, by the military-industrial complex. The potential for the disastrous rise of misplaced power exists and will persist. (Dwight D. Eisenhower, January 17, 1961)

The fuel consumed by the Pentagon in a single year would run the entire U.S. public transit system for 22 years. For the cost of one stealth bomber ($516 million), we could construct 9285 units of housing for low-income families, the elderly, and the handicapped. The world's annual military budget equals the income of 2.6 billion people in the 44 poorest nations. Military defense budgets in the Third World are about seven times as large as in 1960. More wars were fought in 1987 than in any previous year on record; four fifths of the deaths in those wars were civilian.

Worldwide, nations devote an outrageous amount of their resources to the military sector, both to dominate other nations as well as to protect themselves. This massive diversion of the earth's limited resources, nearly one trillion dollars per year, involves nearly all nations, draining funds for internal development and basic human services. The competition between the United States and the Soviet Union has provided the major impetus for the arms race. The most rapid growth in military spending with the most pernicious consequences, however, has taken place in the Third World countries, where military outlays have increased sevenfold since 1960.

The U.S. government today is aligned with people and governments all over the world who want to keep power and wealth in the hands of the few. This policy is necessary to protect U.S. transnational global interests. Unfortunately for the majority of the people of the world, East-West conflicts have been effectively used by the U.S. military-industrial complex to obtain billions of dollars from U.S. taxpayers to maintain the injustices and privileges of the existing global economic order.

D. Economic Dislocation

[Minimum wage] $3.35 an hour jobs don't come near to providing even the basics for three kids. I've been working enough of them to know. (Selena Barr, mother of three from North Carolina)

In 1968, full-time employment at minimum wage resulted in an income slightly above the poverty level for a family of three. In 1988, full-time minimum wage employment yielded 74 percent of the poverty income level for a family of three.

In recent years, Americans have experienced the meaning of such terms as "economic dislocation," "capital flight," and "plant closures" as the character of the U.S. economy has been changed from a leading manufacturing to a corporate service economy. Since reaching a peak in 1973, real U.S. wages declined by 15 percent. The congressional Joint Economic Committee reports that 60 percent of all jobs created since 1979 pay less than $7000 a year. Thus, government statistics are misleading, causing one to assume incorrectly that Americans have benefited by greater employment. Once the largest creditor nation, by 1986 the United States was the largest debtor nation. In the course of these major structural changes, declining farm prices and land values and the displacement of farmers by agribusiness in rural areas threaten to end widespread ownership of agricultural land by productive working farm families. Unregulated movement of jobs and capital between regions and across countries results in factory closings that leave individual workers without jobs and whole communities without a means of livelihood.

In the global economy many of these trends are accentuated. The internationalization of capital and the global scope of operations of transnational corporations give developing countries little control over major disruptions of their economies. Economic problems, whether recession, inflation, or changes in access to markets, produce a terrible toll in human suffering, particularly in the poorest and most vulnerable economies, and the burden of adjustment falls disproportionately on the poor. Since 1982, debtor countries have been paying more funds in debt servicing than they have received in new loans. In 1987, this negative capital flow exceeded 29 billion dollars.

E. Environmental Pollution and Resource Depletion

> *During the next three decades [humankind] will drive an average of 100 species to extinction everyday, . . . The present rate is at least 1,000 times the pace that has prevailed since prehistory. Even the mass extinctions 65 million years ago that killed off the dinosaurs and countless other species did not significantly affect flowering plants. . . But these plant species are disappearing now, and people, not comets or volcanos, are the angels of destruction. Moreover, the earth is suffering the decline of entire ecosystems– the nurseries of new life-forms. . . . British ecologist Norman Myers has called it the "greatest single setback to life's abundance and diversity since the first flickerings of life almost 4 billion years ago." (Time Magazine, January 2, 1989)*

A century of haphazardly producing and disposing of toxic wastes now endangers the earth's rivers, lakes, oceans, and air. Acid rain from the burning of fossil fuels imperils lakes, rivers, and forests, and comprises a health risk in some areas. Nuclear accidents and nuclear wastes threaten the life-supporting capacity of the earth. Increases in carbon dioxide levels from the burning of fossil fuels appear to be creating a global greenhouse effect that will significantly alter climatic conditions.

In 1987, the World Commission on Environment and Development commented that "humanity has the ability to make development sustainable—to ensure that it meets the needs of the present without compromising the ability of future generations to meet their own needs. The concept of sustainable development does imply limits . . . but sustainable development requires meeting the basic needs of all and extending to all the opportunity to fulfil their aspiration for a better life. A world in which poverty is endemic will always be prone to ecological and other catastrophes."

F. Powerlessness

When I give food to the poor they call me a saint, when I ask why the poor have no food, they call me a communist. (Dom Helder Camara, when Archbishop of Recife, Brazil)

In the years since the inception of the global debt crisis, the standard of living has sharply deteriorated in most Third World countries. Do we dare ask why?

Standards of living in the poorest countries have fallen further behind during the last ten years as the global debt crisis has caused a devastating impact on debtor countries. Per capita consumption among the 17 most debt-troubled nations has fallen by 11 percent since 1980. A number of the poorest debtor countries have seen their real incomes plunge by as much as two thirds during this period. Children are the first and most vulnerable victims. UNICEF estimates that 40,000 children die every day from malnutrition and easily preventable diseases. Schools and health clinics are closing because of cuts in government social spending and the high cost of imported supplies.

At the global level the emergence of a global economy characterized by mutual interdependence and shared problems has not been accompanied by the creation of institutions and processes for dealing with these new economic realities. Poor countries are caught in a spiral of unstable and frequently declining prices for the agricultural commodities they export, with limited access to markets in industrialized countries, capital for investment, or new technology. The result is massive indebtedness of many Third World countries that further increases their vulnerability because even small changes in global interest rates or prices can change drastically their economic prospects. Moreover, the global debt crisis has eroded the sovereignty of indebted countries by giving the International Monetary Fund the power to demand major structural reforms and stringent austerity programs as the condition for extending financing to meet interest and debt payments.

Within the United States, many families and individuals feel they have little control over their own economic future. Distant economic policies and events result in high inflation or unemployment and threaten income security. Corporate decisions often have enormous impact on not only the workplace but entire communities. Indeed, we now live in an age when many middle-class families find it increasingly difficult to balance the budget, and the poor live in an even more precarious situation in which any unforeseen economic problem may leave them homeless. In addition to homelessness, this has meant loss of health insurance coverage, family farm foreclosures, declining quality of life, an environment whose very ability to sustain life is threatened by human disasters and many other forms of what the Reverend Jesse Jackson termed "economic violence." Rising housing prices provide wealth to current homeowners, but exclude younger families from home ownership. A sense of economic helplessness creates stress and induces passivity, leading people to drop out of active participation in the social, political, and economic organization of their communities.

V. The Market Economy: Promises and Problems

As Christians we are called to participate in God's reign, by reshaping our human household in the light of our vision of a just economy. Through our covenant with God, we are responsible to God and to our sisters and brothers for the justice of the economic institutions in which we participate. That accountability is even greater in a democratic system through which each citizen retains the political voice to challenge harmful policies and to promote justice. In confronting and confessing the injustices that exist within our own economic institutions, we also express our conviction that God works with and through us to create a more just economic order.

Members of the United Church of Christ are part of a market-oriented economy and citizens of an industrialized capitalist nation that shapes and often dominates the global market economy. We must name and challenge the economic injustices that exist within the United States economic institutions and practices, not because we prefer an alternative form of economic organization, but because this is our household. It is where our responsibilities lie as North American Christians.

A market economy has certain strengths and certain weaknesses. Among the strengths of a market economy are:

1. Markets are especially useful, given the limitations of human beings to foresee all the consequences of actions and complex policies. The price system is more sensitive to shifts in supply and demand than is centralized planning. Resource allocation and reallocation is more flexible and nuanced, and often, more efficient.

2. Combined with a democratic political system, the market economy provides enormous freedom of choice for those who are able to participate in it fully. Those with the resources to purchase goods have a wide selection from which to decide. Those with access to education and training can choose their careers freely. When large numbers of persons participate as equals in the market, power and decision making are dispersed. There is some empirical evidence that states with genuine political liberties are market oriented, although the reverse is not true.

3. Market economies are typically very productive. The profit incentives embedded in a market system encourage the production of a wide range of goods and services. Incentives always exist for producers to increase their productivity through new technologies and more efficient use of workers and machines. Even a number of predominantly nonmarket economies, such as China, have recognized the advantage of allowing some competitive market forces to operate and provide vigor to the economic life of their nation.

4. A long history of economic growth and rising standards of living in market economies testify to the advantages of the market system for at least a portion of the population. In the United States since World War II, average hourly earnings adjusted for inflation have increased by 60 percent. However, it is also true that since 1970 average hourly earnings have been largely stagnant; increases in household income have occurred only because of an increase in the number of workers in the average household. In Japan and many of the market economies of Europe, capitalism combined with government policies have produced even higher rates of growth and higher and more widely distributed standards of living.

Juxtaposed against the vision of God's household, the suffering within our own household demonstrates that we face serious economic problems which markets have not alleviated. Not all of these problems are the direct result of the market system. Many of them result from the interactions of our market economy with a host of humanly constructed social and political institutions. Beyond this, Christian faith affirms that there are other factors than market factors which should motivate our economy, and other claims upon us, including the claims of conscience and of righteousness.

Standing beside the strengths of a market economy are these weaknesses:

1. The market system does not guarantee that the minimum resources needed to fulfill basic human needs will be available to all citizens. Market exchange cannot guarantee equity of social justice. In fact, when combined with already existing inequities of wealth or competence or other forms of social power, market exchange can become, for many, an exchange of desperation. Those who are excluded from or unable to participate in the labor market–particularly children, the elderly, the handicapped, and persons with inadequate skills–typically experience poverty, poor health, and inadequate housing. Even some who work full time in the United States do not earn enough for adequate survival. Experience has demonstrated that economic growth

alone is not enough to alleviate this problem. For instance, steady economic growth over the past five years has not reduced the poverty rate among minorities, and has not increased the earning power of many low-skilled workers.

2. Market exchange cannot count nonmonetary costs, and much of the vaunted efficiency of markets fails when a full cost-accounting does not occur. These uncounted costs, from pollution to the damage done to communities through capital movement, must be dealt with and compensated outside of the market.

3. Unchecked exchange leads not only to gross inequalities of income and wealth but also to concentration of economic power without adequate public accountability. These concentrations of power not only distort the price-system but also encroach on government, the courts, educational institutions, and the family. For instance, the size and the economic resources of large transnational corporations provide them with some degree of independence from national government boundaries. Even within industrialized societies where national governments have regulated certain aspects of corporate behavior with varying degrees of success, regional administrations, local communities, and employees often have little influence on corporate behavior. Problems of public control and corporate accountability are magnified in poor countries, where the size and resources of transnational corporations often exceed that of the state.

4. A market economy emphasizes individual choice and often ignores the importance of public concerns. On the one hand, individual choices are shaped and bounded by the community environment in which they are made. For instance, within a corporate setting individuals often see only certain actions as acceptable or possible. An analysis that emphasizes individual choice but ignores the effects of the larger community upon that choice is fundamentally flawed. On the other hand, an emphasis solely on individual action ignores the importance of considering the welfare of the entire economic household. The Christian message

clearly states that self-interest is not an adequate approach to all economic decisions. There are times when the needs of the larger community, whether that be a family, a church, or a nation, must take precedence over self-interest.

5. Market exchange is, by itself, indifferent to what is exchanged, and market systems will respond to military spending as well as the demand for Barbie dolls. A growing proportion of the budgets of both richer and poorer nations, a total of 15 trillion dollars since 1960, is going into military spending and away from human development. In a similar manner, the international market for illegal drugs responds to a demand, but produces materials that destroy human beings. Deciding what should be produced and what should not requires social decision as well as individual decision. Moreover, protecting nonmarket spheres of life, such as family privacy, requires external restraint.

6. Market exchange encourages a society of mobility and consumption, often corrosive of community values. Although it is true of other economies as well, market economies especially encourage false values and priorities. The accumulation of individual wealth and corporate profit is frequently the ultimate measure of success. This tempts people into believing that the accumulation of things is a primary measure of human worth and stature.

7. In the international arena, where markets often have even fewer restraints, the preceding effects are often exacerbated. The global market economy demonstrates even more clearly its inability to provide for the equitable distribution of resources. Although enough food can be produced worldwide for all humans to have a sufficient diet, serious problems of hunger and malnutrition exist around the world. The market does little to encourage the sharing and cooperation that would result in a better distribution of the world's resources. Many economic problems, such as pollution, labor migration, and international investment flows, are not limited by national boundaries. Economic policy decisions made by large nations such as the United States impact not only their own citizens, but have major

effects on the lives of people around the globe who have little input into those decisions. Existing economic institutions cannot adequately respond to these cross-national economic forces.

These standard defects vary in their impact on different historical circumstances. In the United States they are exacerbated by historical patterns of racism and sexism and other forms of exclusion. Institutional prejudices, for example, racism and sexism, limit the extent to which "free choice" actually operates for individuals of a different race, sex, religion, sexual orientation, or nationality. Thus some people are consistently excluded from full participation in the economic household of our nation. Given the already alarming inequity of income and wealth, and the extraordinary numbers of marginal persons in our society, considerable restructuring must take place for even minimal justice. Moreover, the inequities and exclusion result in part from structural decisions already in effect, for example, the "planned economy" of military expenditures, tax policies transferring income to corporations and other concentrations of economic power, the current incentives for corporate takeovers, and the penalizing of corporate savings and productive investment.

VI. Statement of Christian Conviction

The UCC Statement of Mission reads: "Empowered by the Holy Spirit, we are called and commit ourselves . . . to praise God, confess our sin, and joyfully accept God's forgiveness."

In that spirit, the members of the United Church of Christ, its instrumentalities, local churches, associations, conferences, and all national bodies confess that we live in a privileged society which has committed economic injustices in this nation and the world. We are called to confess that from places of privilege it is difficult to stand in solidarity with the poor and the oppressed.

We are called to confess that we have done too little to correct the economic injustices in the world.

We are called, in the Statement of Mission, to "name

and confront the powers of evil within and among us." One of those powers is the worship of mammon (wealth) in all its forms, to which we have fallen prey.

Similarly, we are called to "repent our silence and complicity with the forces of chaos and death." Our silence and complicity contribute to the economic oppression of persons whom God loves.

Furthermore, we are called to live out the commandment of Jesus: "You shall love the Lord your God with all your heart, and with all your soul, and with all your mind, and with all your strength, . . . you shall love your neighbor as yourself [Mark 12:29–31]." Love for our neighbor compels us to act.

As we confess and repent, we declare our intention to work and struggle for a nation and a world in which every human being is empowered to live life fully, joyfully, and in dignity.

A. Marks of a Just Economy

We affirm that to be involved in the transformation of economic life is an authentic Christian calling. Christ calls the church to bear witness to God's sovereignty and presence among us. Christ calls us from the idolatries of greed and materialism to a full relationship with God, creation, and one another. Christ reveals God's suffering passion with the poor and uncovers God's reign of justice in our midst. In the practice of justice in the public economy the covenant of the human household with God is fulfilled and God is worshiped. Economic justice in God's household includes the following dimensions. They provide a standard by which to measure contemporary economic systems, as well as a vision which can guide and inspire efforts to create greater economic justice in today's world.

1. A just economy celebrates and serves the fundamental covenant purpose of human life, which is to love God and neighbor. The laws of economics are ultimately accountable to the law of God's love. The rules of the marketplace are not autonomous, but they are accountable to God's grace. Human beings do not live by bread alone. In view of the household God is seeking to create, the value of one's life is not measured by one's material possessions.

2. A just economy gives all persons access to the basic material necessities of life. When some people are excluded from the abundance of life which God intends for all persons, justice is denied. From its beginning the household of Jesus Christ has witnessed many evidences of injustice, including large numbers of people in need, and great gaps between rich and poor.

3. A just economy builds and enhances human communities of dignity and well-being. Only in actual human communities are mutual interdependence and dignity recognized. Economic policy should therefore serve to protect and strengthen such community. In a just economy, the division of labor reflects our mutual interdependence and underscores the importance of the participation of all human beings in the community. According to the new covenant in Christ, all individuals are committed to the well-being of the human household as part of their commitment to God.

4. A just economy is inclusive, involving all able people in responsible, participatory, and economically rewarding activity. Excluded from productive and meaningful work and from the means of life, neither the individual nor the community can survive. Hence in a just economy, no one is unfairly disadvantaged or excluded from productive activity. Economic decision making should reflect the needs and participation of all members of the community.

5. A just economy encourages creativity, skill, and diligence. Human productivity and a sense of vocation benefits all of society and provides a sense of accomplishment to individuals. The economic system should call forth the creative and creating nature of human beings.

6. A just economy assures equality of opportunity. Discrimination of any sort, whether based on such factors as race, class, age, ethnic origins, sexual orientation, physical disability, religion, or gender, contradicts the fundamental

Christian affirmation of the equality and worth of all human beings. Discrimination denies the inclusiveness of the human community. When inequality and prejudice are embedded in societal and institutional processes, this constitutes a form of social sin. Justice requires a commitment to affirmative action and structural changes that redress the effects of discrimination, domination, and exploitation.

7. A just economy reflects God's passion for the poor and disadvantaged, enhancing the life opportunities of the poor, the weak, and groups at the margin of society. Indeed, in a truly just economy there will be no poor. Economic resources should be so distributed that all individuals are empowered to participate fully in the economic system. A just economy seeks continually to redress imbalances in wealth and power so that the poor and weak can take control of their lives and shape their own future.

8. A just economy recognizes the integrity, fullness, and sacredness of creation. Economic justice is understood to include environmental wholeness and an ethic that will ensure a sustainable future for the planet. Humanity is an integral part of an interrelated creation. To abuse, exploit, and deplete resources or cause species' extinction for economic gain violates the integrity of creation, and, therefore, is an act of destruction. With time, there will likely be few survivors of major sustained ecological abuse.

9. A just economy acknowledges the dignity of human beings as made known in Jesus Christ, and guarantees the basic human rights necessary to maintain the sacredness of individuals. Human dignity involves the recognition of each person as a decision maker in the community, so that no one is deprived of an active voice. This means recognizing rights to political liberty and participation, and economic rights to food, shelter, and health care.

10. A just economy requires and promotes international peace and well-being. There is no genuine peace without justice, nor can there be justice without peace. In a just economy, the intent of production should center on improving the lives of all citizens, and not on the proliferation of weapons.

B. Implications

Confronted by the suffering and inadequacies of our current economy, we are impelled toward change, seeking to bring greater justice into our economic household. Many of us are deeply troubled by the economic inequities we see within our nation and the world, but also deeply fearful of what greater economic equity and justice might mean for our own lives. We are unwilling to depend upon God alone for our security, and are frightened that economic reform might mean less economic security for ourselves. Some who have been successful in the market economy may find it difficult to acknowledge that the very system that brought them rewards has treated others unjustly. Some whose economic situation is precarious may fear that change will only make things worse. Many would happily vote for reform if it meant that the poor would become middle-income, but are afraid that it might mean instead that the middle-income will become poor. All of these fears we must honestly bring before God. We must confess our lack of faith and ask God's help in overcoming our fears. We must center our lives in God's abundant love. Through worship, praise, and prayer we can find the faith and courage that will enable us to fulfill our covenant with God, working toward an economy in which justice and peace prevail.

With a more faith-centered spirituality we prepare ourselves to seek actively both the cost and the joy of discipleship affirmed in the United Church of Christ Statement of Faith. As individuals this means evaluating our own lifestyles, to see if they are consistent with shared life in the household of God. We must find ways to educate and inform ourselves on the economic suffering of our neighbors and on possible ways in which we can help prevent such suffering in the future. An important part of this education involves talking with those whose economic perspectives differ from our own. We must actively seek out and openly listen to those who are the widow, the orphan, and the sojourner of our day. The church is an important place in which this listening can occur, for it is the one place where people from all economic backgrounds gather together around the table in complete equality before God.

Changes in our own individual lives, however, while a crucial and necessary step, are not enough. Major institutional changes must also occur in the economy of our nation as well. While recognizing the strengths of the market, we must also realize its limits. We must develop mechanisms within the political system which supplement and reform some aspects of the market economy, rectifying economic injustices and increasing the ability of all individuals to be full economic participants. This requires joining together in citizen action. We recognize that there is no clear or easy way to move from biblical and theological mandates to particular policy recommendations. Yet we strongly affirm the following political and economic changes which address some of the injustices and problems in our current economy. We acknowledge that long-term efforts will be necessary to implement these approaches.

1. In order to create a country in which the promise of life, liberty, and the pursuit of happiness is fulfilled for each person, we are committed to achieving an economic "bill of rights" that will provide:

- A guaranteed national minimum income level, ensuring every person access to adequate food, clothing, and shelter;
- A nondiscriminatory national health care program available to all persons;
- A quality education system that provides to every person nurture, enrichment, and education from infancy to adulthood;
- A right to employment consistent with each person's potential;
- A guaranteed right of every person to access housing that is permanent and affordable.

2. To further the promotion of human rights on a global level, we affirm the need for the implementation of the Universal Declaration of Human Rights, endorsed by the United States 40 years ago, which calls all countries to

recognize the economic, human, and political rights of their citizens. To this end, we reiterate the appeal that the U.S. government ratify the Covenant on Economic, Social, and Cultural Rights and other human rights' conventions approved by the United Nations that are pending before the Senate.

3. To create a more democratic economic system in which all people participate and through which all are nurtured, we affirm the need for wider participation in ownership and management of economic institutions and for more inclusive and democratic patterns of decision making in private and public organizations. Economic democracy may include greater use of democratic planning at local and national levels, as well as greater opportunities for worker participation in workplace decisions. Economic democracy also involves facilitating and empowering the poor, racial and ethnic peoples, women, low-income and disempowered groups to participate on a more equal basis in the political decision-making process. Further, economic democracy entails framing economic issues in ways that informed citizens can consider policy alternatives, make intentional decisions, and express their views.

4. We affirm the need to reorder national and global priorities away from military expenditures and toward a just peace economy, as stated in the *Just Peace Pronouncement* adopted by the Fifteenth General Synod. The ending of the cold war now enhances the feasibility of moving from a national security to a just peace economy in which the promotion of human welfare and the elimination of poverty are our primary goals.

5. We affirm the need for public and private sector initiatives that encourage the development of community-based enterprises for creating jobs by meeting local needs such as housing and recreation, and which are accountable to local residents and organizations. Such community development corporations can be funded by government sources or by religious, labor, or other nonprofit groups which may have endowment funds or pension funds to invest.

6. We affirm the need for the development of mechanisms that increase the public accountability and responsibility of corporations and governmental agencies involved in economic decision making.

7. We affirm the need to improve environmental stewardship by the United States and other countries to assure that economic development does not poison the rich abundance of creation for short-term monetary gain. Better stewardship entails intentional and consistent efforts to consider the long-term environmental implications in all economic planning and development and to take measures to protect our fragile ecosystem. Responsible stewardship also requires legally enforceable programs that regulate the use and disposal of toxic wastes and industrial hazards. We additionally support investment in the development and adoption of more sustainable technologies compatible with the needs of future generations. We support the need to strengthen cross-national organizations in their capacity to deal with global environmental issues.

8. We affirm the need for the entire global community to strengthen global economic institutions or establish new ones that will address cross-national economic concerns. In particular,

    a. World economic institutions, such as the International Monetary Fund or the International Bank for Reconstruction and Development, should be restructured to include greater participation on the part of poorer nations in their decisions, so that these institutions reflect the perspectives and needs of the poorer nations as well as the interests of richer countries;

    b. New economic and financial institutions need to be developed to reach and empower the poor more directly;

    c. More rational and equitable strategies should be designed to deal with debt problems at home and abroad. For developing countries this includes shifting the burden from the poor and sharing the responsibility for repayment more equitably among international banks, governments of the industrialized countries, and multilateral economic institutions. Such mechanisms could include ceilings on debt service based on ability to pay, refinancing arrangements to reduce repayment burdens, debt reduction, and major debt elimination in the poorest countries. The inability of poor nations to repay debt should not lead to exploitation by creditor nations;

d. Institutions should be developed that provide international regulation of the behavior of transnational private corporations and that support individual countries in their oversight of these organizations;

e. Equitable and secure ways of funding international institutions need to be actively pursued that will provide resources to address international problems and needs.

Certainly, judged against the vision of justice in the household of God, all current economic systems fall short and are unjust. These affirmations suggest a direction through which our existing economic systems can be transformed. We recognize that these affirmations, if implemented, would only be first steps toward full economic justice. Taken with God's help, they will move us closer to a household in which all may find abundance. As we progress in this struggle, however, we will necessarily recognize new and additional tasks that need to be undertaken and that demand our attention and support. The church should be actively involved in envisioning ways in which greater economic justice can be achieved.

Called by Christ to participate in God's reign, the church must take a leadership role in the movement toward greater economic justice for the whole human household. Thus, the church must become a model of economic justice in its own institutional practices. This will require reviewing and reforming its internal economy to reflect an active concern with issues of economic equity and justice, supporting the struggles of the poor throughout the world, and encouraging the formation of Christian communities which practice resource sharing and income equity and which encourage advocacy and action with the poor.

The church should also invite Christians to review and reform their own individual lives, taking God's grace and God's reign as the central source and purpose of life.

Finally, the church must continue to affirm the vision of justice and peace to which all faithful Christians are called. It must actively preach God's reign of suffering love within the human household. Within the church, individuals and groups from different economic backgrounds can worship together as equals with a common confession to one faith. The church provides a place where reconciliation and recognition of common interests can begin to emerge. The Proposal for Action which accompanies this Pronouncement provides a plan whereby the United Church of Christ can begin to implement this vision.

A Proposal for Action on Christian Faith: Economic Life and Justice

This is the text of the Proposal for Action passed by General Synod 17 of the United Church of Christ in July 1989 to implement the preceding Pronouncement.

I. Summary

This Proposal for Action affirms the United Church of Christ's commitment to be actively concerned with justice in our economic institutions and daily economic lives. It delineates the strategies and specific actions by which all parts of the United Church of Christ (individuals, local churches, instrumentalities, Conferences, Associations and seminaries) can work for economic justice as an imperative of our affirmation and understanding of the Christian faith.

II. Background Statement

This Proposal for Action is based on the proposed *Pronouncement on Christian Faith: Economic Life and Justice.* The proposed *Pronouncement on Christian Faith: Economic Life and Justice* is a synthesis of two proposed *Pronouncements* submitted to the Seventeenth General Synod. This Proposal has been developed in response to the request of the Fourteenth General Synod to engage in a study of economics and theology, and to recommend an appropriate response by the United Church of Christ.

The proposed *Pronouncement on Christian Faith and Economic Life* has been informed by feedback to the study paper, *Christian Faith and Economic Life,* provided by a diverse group of United Church of Christ members. The racial and ethnic members of the United Church of Christ felt that the issue of racism in the context of envisioning appropriate economic life from a Christian faith perspective needed further articulation; this was provided in the proposed *Pronouncement on Christian Faith and Economic Jus-*

tice. The Seventeenth General Synod celebrates the active involvement of diverse groups in the discussion and formulation of proposed statements on the highly complex issues of Christian faith and economics presented in these two documents. Hence, the Seventeenth General Synod celebrates the fulfillment of the United Church of Christ's motto: "That they may all be one."

The synthesized *Pronouncement* presents policy statements for the United Church of Christ on the issue of economic justice. This Proposal for Action, therefore, delineates a specific program of action strategies that will enable the United Church of Christ to become effectively involved at all levels in the struggle to ensure that economic justice is a reality for all of God's people in the United States and throughout the world.

This Proposal for Action further seeks to implement, through Christian social action, the programmatic thrust of the *Pronouncement on Christian Faith: Economic Life and Justice* which seeks to remain faithful to the Statement of Faith and the Statement of Mission of the United Church of Christ.

III. Directional Statements and Goals

"God calls the worlds into being, creates persons in God's image, and sets before each one the ways of life and death . . . "

Our lives are derived from and lived in relationship with God. Our joy is to live in covenant with God and one another in God's household. Our delight is to use freely and faithfully the gifts of God who is Creator.

"In Jesus Christ, the man of Nazareth, our crucified and risen Savior, God has come to us . . . "

As people of the United Church of Christ, affirming our Statements of Faith and Mission, we seek within the Church Universal to participate in God's mission of economic justice for all of God's peoples and to follow the liberating way of the crucified and risen Christ . . .

We have confessed and stated our Christian conviction to struggle against all forms of economic injustice in this nation and throughout the world . . .

We establish as a goal the just transformation of the market economy into an economic system that fundamentally ensures economic, environmental, gender, racial, and social justice and equality in the United States . . .

We further establish as a goal the just transformation of the global economy into an economic order that fundamentally ensures economic, environmental, gender, racial, and social justice for all of God's peoples throughout the world . . .

To acknowledge God's reign is to shape on earth a community capable of the humanity exemplified in Jesus Christ and to take the suffering love of God made known in the life, crucifixion, and resurrection of Jesus as the model for a covenant household of justice and love. Thus, God's reign does not mean to flee the rigors of earth and seek some heavenly holiness, rather is sought through service, advocacy, and covenant.

Based on this confession and affirmation, the Seventeenth General Synod calls for the adoption of the following actions.

IV. Call to Members

The Seventeenth General Synod calls members to develop a faith-oriented understanding of economic life by engaging in

1. Regular public worship, the center and foundation of Christian life, which renews our covenant with God to seek justice in God's household;

2. Prayer and spiritual discipline, to strengthen the struggle for economic justice, which includes tithing or giving to share resources with those who have less;

3. Theological reflection on the basic tenets of Christian faith to understand better the imperatives of God's mission of economic justice;

4. Efforts to adopt a personal and family lifestyle consistent with life in the household of God and God's creation;

5. Personal contact with and listening to individuals of other races, classes, income levels, economic backgrounds, and nationalities;

6. Personal initiatives and voluntary service to promote economic justice, including involvement in the political process.

V. Call to Local Churches

The Seventeenth General Synod calls local churches and their members to respond to the call for economic justice in their worship and education activities, financial decisions, and social outreach.

1. **Worship and Spiritual Concerns:** We call churches to
   a. Preach on God, giver of abundant creation, who is a lover of justice and creation, and on the justice-seeking ministry of Christ. This includes regularly incorporating visions of economic justice into public worship;
   b. Encourage all members to pray, meditate, and engage in those spiritual disciplines that help relate Christian faith to economic life;
   c. Minister to and support those members struggling to live just Christian lives in their work environments, as well as those members and families who are struggling to transform their personal lifestyles and commitments to be more consistent with seeking justice and wholeness in God's household.
   d. Implement a program of Christian education that informs and challenges us to knowledge of economic injustices and to commitments to develop more just economic structures and systems.

2. **Study and Education:** We call churches to engage in study and educational programming that will enable their members better to reflect on and act for economic justice. We call churches to
   a. Establish study groups to engage in Bible study, and to utilize the foregoing *Pronouncement*, the study paper *Christian Faith and Economic Life,* and other documents

that relate Christian faith to economic life and the economy of the environment;

b. Study the economy of their local communities, analyze local economic inequities and injustices, identify the social forces, conditions and the policies which contribute to economic suffering, and explore ways their church can address these problems. This may include providing opportunities for dialogue between people of different economic backgrounds;

c. Seek out churches of different racial and economic backgrounds and engage in study and dialogue with them on issues of economic justice;

d. Increase members' awareness of global economic issues and the concerns and perspectives of persons around the world on these issues. This may include explicitly studying the differing views of the advantages and disadvantages of the market economy held by people who have suffered or benefitted from the promises and problems of the market;

e. Support and encourage church members regarding their own economic pain and problems.

3. An Economic Audit of the Church: We call local churches to examine critically the economy of their own church. We call churches to

a. Invest church endowment funds and other church investments in a manner consistent with the economic justice commitments of the United Church of Christ. This means careful attention to the policies of the financial managers, the financial institutions, and the issuers of securities that are selected, as well as active monitoring of the investment decisions made by church managers and/or church oversight committees;

b. Examine the extent to which the church budget provides equitably for the salaries, pensions, and benefits of all church staff;

c. Examine and make sure that the church budget reflects a serious commitment to promote economic justice in the community and the world;

d. Study and adopt procedures in the institutional lifestyle of the church that are consistent with life in the household of God, including regular self-examination of the extent to which the church is focusing on acquisitive and materialistic patterns of behavior, often reflected in an overemphasis on such items as cushions, carpets, or organs;

e. Implement just church policies for hiring and firing of staff, with particular attention to the hiring of minorities and women;

f. Examine purchasing practices with attention to the equal employment and affirmative action practices of suppliers and vendors;

g. Audit church property and equipment for responsible energy use, resource conservation, recycling practices, sound land use, and less polluting forms of transportation.

4. Advocacy for Economic Justice: We call local churches to

a. Join and participate actively in the Justice and Peace Network of the United Church of Christ, and the Network for Environmental and Economic Responsibility, and in interfaith advocacy organizations such as IMPACT and Interfaith Action for Economic Justice;

b. Work on economic injustices within the local community and support community organizations that enhance the life opportunities and political voice of poor and minority groups, and that increase local economic control;

c. Interpret, support, and participate in the work for economic justice conducted by the Conferences, and the national boards and instrumentalities of the United Church of Christ.

VI. Call to United Church of Christ Instrumentalities, Conferences, Associations and Seminaries

The Seventeenth General Synod calls national United Church of Christ instrumentalities, Conferences, Associations, and the closely related seminaries of the United Church of Christ to respond to the call for economic justice through education, institutional change, and advocacy.

1. The Economy of the United Church of Christ: We call the United Church of Christ to work for economic justice by transforming its own internal organizational structure to conform to life in the household of God, so it reflects a commitment to economic justice. We call the United Church of Christ to

a. Establish or commission existing committees for economic justice at the Association and Conference levels;

b. Sponsor research and development of a critical analysis of current economic justice issues and make recommendations for economic structures and systems that ensure economic justice for all people;

c. Examine and, where appropriate, encourage change in the distribution of income and resources among Conferences and Associations as well as between wealthier and poorer churches, seeking greater sharing based on mission and need;

d. Continue to promote socially responsible investment of the endowments and pensions of congregations, Conferences, and instrumentalities. Where appropriate to the charter of the investment funds, the United Church of Christ should encourage greater use of investments that address economic justice objectives, but may entail greater risk or lower yields;

e. Examine equity in salaries, pensions, and benefits paid to United Church of Christ employees, and design structures that address current inequities;

f. Establish national and regional programs and projects that seek economic justice in the United States and in the world;

g. Assure that policies for hiring and firing of staff are just with particular attention to the hiring of minorities and women;

h. Confront racism and sexism within the church, strengthening the affirmative action activities of the denomination;

i. Reorient the interpretation, promotion, funding patterns, and priorities of mission programs to reflect the United Church of Christ's commitment to economic justice;

j. Develop ways to involve more people from the local church level, particularly from poor and minority communities, in the decision-making and budgeting process of the denomination.

2. Study and Education:

a. We call upon all Instrumentalities and other national bodies to research and publish critical and constructive analysis of present economic structures and systems and make recommendations for just economic structures and systems;

b. We call closely related seminaries of the United Church of Christ to participate in the development of a theology which demonstrates the relevance of biblical faith to economic systems and practices in the world and which affirms the wholeness of God's creation. Seminaries should be encouraged to offer courses that give students in the ministry a grounding in economics and economic justice, as well as provide similar continuing education opportunities for clergy and concerned lay people;

c. We call the appropriate United Church of Christ instrumentalities to collect or develop and distribute curriculum materials which foster the study of economic justice issues by youth and adults in local churches;

d. We call the national bodies of the United Church of Christ, along with Conferences and Associations, to develop seminars and other programs that provide for the study of economic justice issues;

e. We call the Office for Church in Society, the United Church Board for World Ministries, the United Church Board for Homeland Ministries, the Commission for Racial Justice, and the Council for Racial and Ethnic Ministries to encourage the study of the *Pronouncement on Christian Faith: Economic Life and Justice* and of supporting documents. These groups are en-

couraged to appoint a task force to expand this pronouncement into a fuller study resource, similar to *A
Just Peace Church*, and, in cooperation with Conferences and Associations, to conduct a church-wide study
process;

f. We call the Stewardship Council to develop a Sunday
bulletin back-page series that tells stories of economic
justice and injustice and relates these issues to biblical
faith, and to utilize other means of communicating
economic justice themes such as Mission Moments
and offering material.

g. We call all bodies of the church to provide for study
opportunities and dialogue which mix people across
economic, racial, and national lines, providing the
opportunity for all groups in the church to listen to
the concerns of those whose perspectives differ.

3. Advocacy for Economic Justice: We call the various bodies of the United Church of Christ, under the leadership of
the Office for Church in Society, to increase their advocacy
efforts on behalf of economic justice in the economic life
of this nation and the international community. We call
OCIS, BWM, BHM, and CRJ to

a. Lobby for legislative efforts that embody the policy
proposals in Section VI of the foregoing *Pronouncement*;

b. Continue efforts to develop the Justice and Peace Network, placing emphasis on issues of economic justice
and their links with peace issues;

c. Initiate efforts to develop an eco-justice advocacy network to address the linkage between economic and
environmental justice issues;

d. Empower churches and individuals to organize effectively and to change conditions of poverty;

e. Gather poor people in conferences and hearings, so
that their stories may be heard within churches, and
the media, and Congress;

f. Continue to advocate divestment from all corporations doing business in South Africa and other nations where economic and racial oppression are com-
monplace;

g. Continue to advocate for the medically indigent and
physically disabled as a result of catastrophic illnesses
such as AIDS.

4. Ecumenical Initiatives: We call the Office of the President to take the initiative in approaching the National Conference of Catholic Bishops and the major Protestant denominations that have written public theologies of economics to discuss the development of an ecumenical statement
on economic justice that would address the nation.

VII. Call to Participation in the Global Community

The Seventeenth General Synod calls upon all members, congregations, Associations, Conferences, instrumentalities, and related institutions in the United Church of
Christ to recognize that we are members of a global community in which a majority of our brothers and sisters are
poor. There is a need within this global community to
create a new household, bearing one another's burdens
and sharing God's gift of life together. To stand with God
in solidarity with all people, particularly the poor and oppressed, and to challenge the value systems of this world,
we call all parts of the United Church of Christ to

1. Recognize the existence of one interdependent and global household and one mutually responsible people. This
includes support of grassroots people's movements involved
in the struggle for justice, peace, and full human development;

2. Participate in extensive people-to-people and congregational exchanges through the United Church Board for
World Ministries, providing direct exposure to the situations and problems of churches and individuals in poorer
countries;

3. Provide greater support to the ministries of partner
churches, social service and relief programs, Christian seminaries, and educational, environmental and health institutions in poorer countries;

4. Participate in and support the World Council of Churches and other international interfaith institutions;

5. Invest in alternative financial institutions, such as the Ecumenical Development Cooperative Society, or other lending arrangements that promote socially desirable goals, such as housing, community economic development, and projects initiated by the poor;

6. Solicit the participation of partner churches into United Church of Christ structures and mission programs;

7. Develop new and more effective programmatic relationships with sisters and brothers in the Third World that enhance the global struggle toward economic justice;

8. Provide national and international leadership toward the development of an effective global ecumenical movement for economic justice which has as its central goal the just transformation of the global economic order.

VIII. Implementation

The Seventeenth General Synod requests that the Office for Church in Society, in consultation with the United Church Board for World Ministries, the United Church Board for Homeland Ministries, the Commission for Racial Justice, and the Council for Racial and Ethnic Ministries, coordinate the implementation of this Proposal for Action through a broadly representative interagency and churchwide committee and make a detailed report to the Eighteenth and succeeding General Synods.

Suggested Further Reading

Books on Faith and Economics

Balasuriya, Tissa. *Planetary Theology*. Maryknoll, N.Y.: Orbis Books, 1984.

Birch, Bruce C., and Larry L. Rasmussen. *The Predicament of the Prosperous*. Philadelphia: Westminster Press, 1978.

Brown, Robert McAfee, and Sydney Thomson Brown, eds. *A Cry for Justice: The Churches and Synagogues Speak*. New York: Paulist Press, 1989.

Duchrow, Ulrich. *Global Economy: A Confessional Issue for the Churches?* Geneva, Switzerland: World Council of Churches Publications, 1986.

Elliott, Charles. *Comfortable Compassion? Poverty, Power and the Church*. New York: Paulist Press, 1987.

Meeks, M. Douglas. *God the Economist*. Minneapolis, Minn: Fortress Press, 1989.

Mulholland, Catherine, ed. *Ecumenical Reflections on Political Economy*. Geneva, Switzerland: World Council of Churches Publications, 1988.

Owensby, Walter L. *Economics for Prophets*. Grand Rapids, Mich: Wm. B. Eerdmans Pub. Co., 1988.

Sider, Ronald J., ed. *Cry Justice: The Bible on Hunger and Poverty*. A Bread for the World Reader. New York, N.Y.: Paulist Press, 1980.

Sider, Ronald J. *Rich Christians in an Age of Hunger*. rev. ed. Downers Grove, Ill: Inter Varsity Press, 1984.

Stivers, Robert L, ed. *Reformed Faith and Economics*. Lanhan, Md: University Press of America, 1989.

Simon, Arthur. *Christian Faith and Public Policy: No Grounds for Divorce*. Grand Rapids, Mich.: Wm. B. Eerdmans Pub. Co., 1987.

Stackhouse, Max L. *Public Theology and Political Economy*. Grand Rapids, Mich: Wm. B. Eerdmans Pub. Co., 1987.

Strain, Charles R., ed. *Prophetic Visions and Economic Realities*. Grand Rapids, Mich.: Wm. B. Eerdmans Pub. Co., 1989.

Wogaman, J. Phillip. *The Great Economic Debate: An Ethical Analysis*. Philadelphia: Westminster Press, 1977.

Books on Economic and Policy Issues

(There are many excellent resources on specific issues. This list includes books that address some of the broader topics.)

Bread for the World Institute on Hunger and Development. *Hunger 1990: A Report on the State of World Hunger.* Washington, D.C.: Bread for the World, 1990.

Carter, Nancy A. *Keeping Covenant with the Poor: Study Guide on Poverty in North America.* New York, N.Y.: Friendship Press, 1988.

Danziger, Sheldon H., and Daniel H. Weinberg. *Fighting Poverty.* Cambridge, Mass.: Harvard University Press, 1986.

Ellwood, David T. *Poor Support: Poverty in the American Family.* New York: Basic Books, 1988.

Forrester, Duncan B., and Danus Skene, eds. *Just Sharing.* London, England: Epworth Press, 1988.

Garfinkel, Irwin, and Sara S. McLanahan. *Single Mothers and Their Children.* Washington, D.C.: The Urban Institute Press, 1986.

Gittings, James A. *Breach of Promise: Portraits of Poverty in North America.* New York: Friendship Press, 1988.

National Research Council. *A Common Destiny: Blacks and American Society.* Washington, D.C.: National Academy Press, 1989.

Simon, Arthur. *Bread for the World.* rev. ed. New York: Paulist Press, 1984.

Sivard, Ruth Leger. *World Military and Social Expenditures, 1989.* Washington, D.C.: World Priorities Council, 1989.

The World Bank. *World Development Report 1990: Poverty.* Oxford, England: Oxford University Press, 1990.

Books on Economics

Blinder, Alan. *Hard Heads, Soft Hearts.* New York: Basic Books, 1988.

Copeland, Warren R. *Economic Justice: The Social Ethics of U.S. Economic Policy.* Nashville: Abingdon Press, 1988.

Galbraith, John K. *Economics in Perspective.* Boston: Houghton Mifflin Co., 1987.

Heilbroner, Robert, and Lester Thurow. *Economics Explained.* New York: Basic Books, 1987.

Hirschman, Albert O. *Rival Views of Market Society.* New York: Viking Press, 1986.

Church Publications

(There are numerous church statements on specific economic policy issues. This is a list of more general statements available on economics and faith.)

Canadian Conference of Catholic Bishops. "A Statement on Social Policy." *Dissent* (Summer 1988): 314-21.

The Episcopal Church in the U.S.A. Urban Bishops Coalition. *Economic Justice and the Christian Conscience.* 1987. (Commended to the Episcopal Church for study by the House of Bishops, 1987.)

National (U.S.) Conference of Catholic Bishops. *Economic Justice for All: Pastoral Letter in Catholic Social Teaching & U.S. Economy.* Washington, D.C.: National Conference of Catholic Bishops, 1986.

Affiliated study guide for *Economic Justice for All.* Joan Marie Maliszewski, John Mitchell Jr., and Patricia Natali, authors. New York: Paulist Press, 1986.

Presbyterian Church, U.S.A. *Christian Faith and Economic Justice.* New York: Office of the General Assembly, 1984. (Approved as a study document at the 196th (1984) General Assembly.)

Presbyterian Church, U.S.A. *Toward a Just, Caring, and Dynamic Political Economy.* New York: The Report of the Committee on a Just Political Economy, Advisory Council on Church and Society, June 1985. New York: Office of the General Assembly, 1985. (Approved as a study document at the 197th (1985) General Assembly.)

United Church of Christ. *Christian Faith and Economic Life.* Audrey Chapman Smock, ed. New York: Hunger Action Office, United Church Board for World Ministries, January 1987. (A study paper distributed to all churches.)

Affiliated study guide for *Christian Faith and Economic Life.* Charles McCollough, author. New York: Hunger Action Office, United Church Board for World Ministries, 1987.

United Church of Christ. *A Pronouncement on Christian Faith: Economic Life and Justice.* Washington, D.C.: Office for

Church in Society, October 1989. (Approved by the 17th General Synod, July 1989, and included as an appendix to this book.)

Affiliated study guide for *A Pronouncement on Christian Faith: Economic Life and Justice.* Charles McCollough, author. Washington, D.C.: Office for Church in Society, 1990.